CRUSH IT!

also by gary vaynerchuk

Gary Vaynerchuk's 101 Wines:
Guaranteed to Inspire, Delight,
and Bring Thunder to Your World

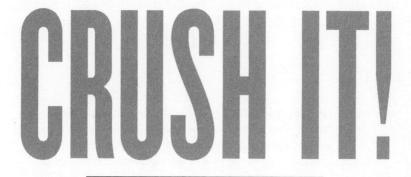

CRUSH IT!

why NOW is the time to
cash in on your passion

gary vaynerchuk

harperstudio

An Imprint of HarperCollins*Publishers*

HarperCollins books may be purchased for educational, business, or sales promotional use. For information please write: Special Markets Department, HarperCollins Publishers, 10 East 53rd Street, New York, NY 10022.

To book Gary Vaynerchuk for a speaking engagement, visit www.harpercollinsspeakers.com.

For more information about this book or other books from Harper-Studio, visit www.theharperstudio.com.

FIRST EDITION

Designed by Cassandra J. Pappas

Library of Congress Cataloging-in-Publication Data has been applied for.

ISBN 978-0-06-191417-1
ISBN 978-0-06-196914-0 (B & N edition)

10 11 12 13   OV/RRD   20 19 18 17 16 15 14 13 12

contents

acknowledgments

This book couldn't have happened without so many people. First and foremost is the wonderful family that surrounds me: My amazing and world-class wife, Lizzie, is my partner in crime and the person whose support allows me to accomplish so much; my parents, Tamara and Sasha, are my whole life and without them I wouldn't be half the man I am; my siblings, Liz and AJ, are my dearest friends and I adored every second growing up with them. And to my other brothers, Alex and Justin, I love you guys! Finally, my new and most amazing love, my newborn, Misha—she has shown me a love I never knew was out there!

After my family there is an amazing team of people who have helped me to do this: Brandon Warnke, my best friend, gave me the freedom to do so much by holding down the Wine Library fort; Bobby Shifrin, my cousin, is more of an older brother and one of my closest friends; Matt Sitomer, my assistant, is a friend and person who really helps me more than anyone on a day-to-day basis and for that I am so grateful—I am truly lucky to have him on my team. Erik Kastner and John Kassimatis showed me the door of the Internet and had a huge impact on my views and I adore them like family.

Finally, the book you are about to read had no prayer of getting in front of you without the amazing team at HarperStudio. The fantastic Debbie Stier saw me speak at a conference and said to herself that she was going to publish me; she was right and her friendship and push and hustle during this process have made this book hers as much as it is mine. Bob Miller's vision supported this project from the very beginning when I first dropped by to hang out in his office. The second I sat down in Austin, Texas, with the fantastic Stephanie Land, I knew she was going to help me write this book. I could see it in her face. I knew my charm and charisma were not going to be enough to win her over, but after she saw I had the chops, she jumped onboard. A super-special thanks to the ladies at The Brooks Group, Caroline, Niki, Erica, and of course Rebecca; you guys are the best and I thank you for your 24/7 efforts. To Peter Klein, not only are you a wonderful father-in-law, but your insights were very helpful. And finally, this would not be the book it is without the thoughtful comments of Travis Kalanick, who gave me the perfect feedback in the late innings.

To all of these people, I am deeply grateful.

CRUSH IT!

---

one

passion is everything

ow badly do you want to crush it? Is it an all-consuming feeling? Do you stay awake at night, your brain swimming with ideas and dreams? Are you willing to do whatever it takes for the chance to live entirely on your own terms? If so, you're lucky. You're lucky because you live in an age of unmatched opportunity for anyone with enough hustle, patience, and big dreams. I should know, since that's all I had to work with.

Three years ago I was an anomaly, a guy with very limited technology skills who used social media sites like Facebook and Twitter and Tumblr to build a highly fulfilling and profitable personal brand. Back then, a lot of people were unwilling to accept that the business world—that society—was changing, and if I had tried to tell you that you could build a business that creates wealth and the most happiness you've ever known with nothing more than passion and a willingness to work your face off, you might not have believed me. Now, though, the opportunities are endless—I don't think enough people have yet grasped just how much society and business and even the Internet have changed—and my story is about to become a lot less unusual. If you want it badly enough, it can become your story, in a lot less time and for a lot less money.

Here's how fast change has taken hold: I helped take my dad's local liquor store, Shopper's Discount Liquors, and blew it up from four million dollars to fifty million dollars in eight years (1998–2005). I'm proud of that. But aside from a ton of hard work, it took millions of dollars in advertising with the *New York Times*, *Wine Spectator*, and other publications as well as radio stations and local TV. Compare that with when I started building my personal brand in February 2006—to this day it has cost me far less in money (less than $15,000) than in sweat, and I'm having more fun than I've ever had in my life. You've got sweat, right? You may not have connections, or an education, or wealth, but with enough passion and sweat, you can make anything happen.

three rules

You may have picked up this book because you want to know the secret to my success. Well, my secret is that I live by three pretty simple rules:

Love your family.
Work superhard.
Live your passion.

That's it. Notice that I don't mention the Internet, or social media tools, or even technology, even though they have been crucial to everything I've accomplished in the last few years. That's because I measure my success by how happy I am, not how big the business is or how much money I've made. And thanks to following those three rules, I'm 100 percent happy.

Don't believe me? Think it's not possible? I promise you it is.

If you don't already live the first principle, get on it, because what I'm going to tell you in this book is worthless if you're not taking care of your family. Your family always comes first. But if you've got that priority straight, and you're working hard, and you're still not 100 percent happy, it's probably because you're not living your passion. And that, my friends, although it is only one-third of the secret to success, is the whole key to staking your claim in the new business world we live in today.

Live your passion. What does that mean, anyway? It means that when you get up for work every morning, every single morning, you are pumped because you get to talk about or work with or do the thing that interests you the most in the world. You don't live for vacations because you don't need a break from what you're doing—working, playing, and relaxing are one and the same. You don't even pay attention to how many hours you're working because to you, it's not really work. You're making money, but you'd do whatever it is you're doing for free.

Does this sound like you? Are you living, or just earning a living? You spend so much time at work, why waste it doing anything other than what you love most? Life is too short for that. You owe it to yourself to make a massive change for the better, and all you have to do is go online and start using the tools waiting for you there.

what you need to know

In this book I'll explain step by step how to use all the social networking tools on the Internet to take whatever it is that rocks your world—the activity that you would do every minute if you could, the topic that you just can't shut up about, the product that you would like to put in everyone's hands—and build it into not just a business but a powerful personal brand that makes you all the money and, more important, brings you all the happiness you could ever want. For those of you already living your passion but hungry to boost your business even further, you'll find some fresh ideas on how to do that, as will anyone interested in developing a strong brand identity for an already existing product or service.

Among the topics we'll cover:

- How to correctly channel your passion into a blog followed by thousands of people interested in consuming your personal brand.
- What real hustle looks like.
- How to get the attention of advertisers itching to give you a portion of their billion dollars in ad revenue.
- Why building a personal brand through social media is crucial to professional survival and advancement, no matter what your field.

- Why you should make plans to grow a business around your personal brand and leave your current job even if you're happily employed.
- How social networking gives you the data you need to find the next social trend and financial opportunity.
- Why savvy social networkers are great cocktail party guests, and how you can become one, too.
- How to monetize your interaction with every person you talk to online.
- The best marketing strategy ever.
- Where to fish for diverse sources of revenue.
- How companies should use social networks to shape their story and strengthen their brand.
- How to build legacy, which is always greater than currency and the mortar to a successful, lasting brand and business.

Social media give entrepreneurs and businesses an unprecedented chance to engage with their customers and communicate their message. Those who can harness their passion to the unbelievable reach and power of these tools are in a position to crush it on a level the world has never seen.

the game has changed

Everyone knows the Internet represents one of the biggest cultural shifts since the printing press, but I think society has been slow to recognize that it represents the biggest shift in history in how we do business. Like, ever. It's matured from a haven for coding geeks to a second home for most Americans, who still spend countless hours shopping online but who are also increasingly moving their social lives there thanks to networking sites like Facebook, YouTube, Flickr, Tumblr, and Twitter. It makes total sense that if this is where the eyeballs are going, this is where business has to go. Money goes where people go—where there is an audience, advertisers are eager to follow. They used to spend their money on traditional media—radio, television, newspapers, and magazines. Those platforms are losing eyeballs to the online world by the second, and many media companies never implemented the leaner, meaner business model they needed to stay alive. They're dead. If the survivors in the traditional media don't adjust to this new competitor, thirty years from now our kids will examine them in museums with the same curiosity they now reserve for dinosaur bones and fossils.

I'm going to make a lot of massive, bold statements in this book, but let me assure you that I'm not trying to be a shock jock. I wouldn't say anything unless I'd thought long and hard about it.

Advertisers and companies need to spend money to stay alive, so why shouldn't they spend it on you? By building a personal brand using social media networks, you're practically doing them a favor. Since the only investment it takes to use these sites to grow a business is ridiculous amounts of time and hustle, these platforms are open to whoever has got the chops to get in the game. That's you, right?

no excuses

But, Gary, some of you might be saying, my passion isn't something cool and retail friendly like wine. I'm into *World of Warcraft*. I'm obsessed with belly dancing. I regularly piss off my wife because I'd rather hole up in the basement with my friends playing cards than do anything else. I want to build a business, but there's no money to be made in that. Plus, I've got rent or a mortgage, kids and elderly parents, student loans and car payments.

Yeah, well, so did Perez Hilton, and Ze Frank and Veronica Belmont, and Heather Cocks and Jessica Morgan (gofugyourself.typepad.com). They totally crushed it, and you can, too. Do it now.

But, Gary, someone else might say, have you kept up with the news over the past few years? The economy has taken a beating, a lot of people have lost jobs, consumers are not spending like they once did, and advertisers are far more conservative than they used to be. I'm reading this book to plan ahead for the day when I know for sure it's a good time to start a business.

It's never a bad time to start a business unless you're starting a mediocre business. I think economic downturns represent a huge opportunity for everyone to get their focus on and start to crush it. The person who can dominate during rough times is the person who can dominate, period. Yes, we've seen a lot of people close up shop in the past years, but if they had offered *a relevant and differentiated product or service,* had been adaptable, and most of all had known how to tell their story, they wouldn't have had to close. I know that's an unpopular thing to say, but

I think once you read further and understand how our culture has changed and what the next generation—whether entrepreneurs or not—needs to do to make its mark, you'll agree with me. Booming economies like the one that recently ended keep all kinds of businesses afloat that should have sunk a long time ago. Once the winds shift, there's only room left for the best. What kind of business did you plan on starting, a mediocre one or one that's kick-ass? You know the right answer. Follow the suggestions laid out in this book and your business will be standing and profitable for as long as you want it to be. Plus, you will have achieved more professional happiness than you ever imagined.

Maybe you're out of work and you're thinking you might dabble with some of the ideas in this book every day after you send out your résumé and make a few calls (the traditional résumé, by the way, is about to become obsolete, but more on that later). Tell me this, though: Did you jump up every morning eager to go to that job you lost? If not, why are you looking for another one just like it? You have an unbelievable opportunity. Use all this extra time you have to reinvent yourself or follow a totally different path from the one you were on before, maybe one where the only thing at the end isn't a custom-engraved watch that reads "Thanks for your service" and a surf-and-turf farewell dinner to send you off into retirement. You can do better so long as you're willing to live and breathe your passion. Do that, and you'll no longer differentiate between your work life and your personal life. You'll just live, and love doing it.

As for those of you still employed, even happily employed, this book is for you, too. Mark my words, if you want to stay relevant and competitive in the coming years—I don't care if you're in sales, tech, finance, publishing, journalism, event planning, business development, retail, service, you name it—you will still need to develop and grow your personal brand. Everyone— EVERYONE—needs to start thinking of themselves as a brand. It is no longer an option; it is a necessity.

My DNA made me want to start businesses and go big and bold and conquer the world and crush the competition and buy the New York Jets, and there are a lot of you reading this book who see what I've done and think, "Yeah, that's awesome!" I've got a lot to share with you. But if that's not you, I think I can still help you out. Maybe your DNA is totally different from mine. You just want to live comfortably, provide for your loved ones, prepare for the future, and not worry too much. You're set. The average U.S. salary is around 40–50K. You can earn that doing a job you love or a job you hate. Please choose love!

Of course money and security matters, and I am very aware that many people live paycheck to paycheck. Let me reiterate that the process I am going to be talking about takes a lot of time, effort, and focus, but not a lot of dollars, if any. That, my friends, is the game changer; everyone has a shot, not just those with extra cash.

Learn to live your passion, and you'll have all the money you need plus total control over your own destiny. That's a pretty comfortable place to be, wouldn't you say?

this means you

What if you just don't have a hard business instinct? Don't worry; skills are cheap, passion is priceless. If you're passionate about your content and you know it and do it better than anyone else, even with few formal business skills you have the potential to create a million-dollar business. Here's why: let's say you love to fish, and you happen to know a load about worms. In fact, you're embarrassed at how much you like worms and like to talk about worms. But there's no way you can make money on worms, right? Wrong. You can use the Internet to build a platform where you can talk about worms to your heart's content. Passion is contagious. If you channel it into creating amazing content and distribute that content using the social media tools I discuss in this book, someone like me who rocks at business development will eventually find it and become a fan. The day I hear you say that you can use a particular kind of worm to catch 80 percent more bass than you might otherwise, I'm going to see the business opportunity and contact you. Together we create an online show or a written blog or an audio podcast around your passion to reach the fishing marketplace, a billion-dollar industry. We launch the content, and people are immediately drawn to you, we build a community by capitalizing on all the social media tools and techniques at our disposal, we work as many hours as possible, and next thing we know we have the biggest fishing lure company in the country asking to advertise on our site. From there we start building word of mouth and opening up more revenue streams, and *ka-ching*! Your passion for worms in tandem with my passion for biz dev will inevitably result in a business that crushes it. Thanks to the accessibility and reach of social media and the zero cost, anyone can do this. Salesman Steve who rocked selling for Blockbuster needs to find One Man

Stan the Fellini fan and build a million-dollar movie-review business. Joanne Jogger who chronicles her marathon training needs to find Marketer Marvin and create a running blog that kills it and attracts Nike as a sponsor. There is room for everyone in the world of social media, which is the same thing as saying that there is room for everyone in today's business world.

Social Media

=

Business.

Period.*

Everybody wins in these scenarios. Stan and Joanne may seem like the big winners because they're enjoying some fame, yet off in the back room, if Steve and Marvin are living their passion, believe me, they're rocking that party hard. In fact, for all the Web fame and national TV appearances and coverage I have received, it's the behind-the-scenes brand building that has given me more happiness than anything else.

Maybe you're reading this and thinking, *Cool, I'm a businessperson, I don't have to think about my passion, I just have to find someone else who's passionate and use their content to create a business.* Maybe. If your passion, your true-blue passion, isn't business development and marketing and sales, you need to figure out what it is and do that instead, otherwise you'll fail. If you do have that passion for biz dev, however, you may not need a partner at all. I didn't.

---

*You want me to explain this global, over-the-top statement in more detail than I have room for in this book? E-mail me at gary@vaynermedia.com.

it's up to you

The messages in this book are timeless: Do what makes you happy. Keep it simple. Do the research. Work hard. Look ahead. Remember that when I started Wine Library TV in 2006, Facebook was still a college play; I didn't want to be the creepy guy peddling wine to underage kids, so I couldn't use it to bring an audience to my online show. Twitter had just been born and no one knew what it was. Once these social networking platforms caught on with the general population, however, I was all over them and knew how to make them work for me; but they only accelerated my success—they didn't create it. Keep that in mind as you start to put your dreams and plans into action. The tools we're going to discuss in this book will spread your ideas and give your personal brand more traction in far less time and for far less money than you might have been able to do otherwise, *but they are only as powerful as the person who uses them.*

Their power is also only as strong as their most recent incarnation. Technology and innovation and consumer demand are working together at such a frenzied pace that by the time you read this book some of the capabilities and reach of these platforms will have already changed. Regardless of what changes we see in the little details in the user interface or individual features of these tools, they won't affect the big picture—you can pimp your ride, but that doesn't change the essence of how you travel in your car. These tools will take you to your audience, where you can follow them, reach out, and make them listen.

I can show you how to use social media to plant a garden or

build a whole new house. Some of you want to be mayor of the whole damn city, and I can help you get there. But no matter how modestly or high you set your sights, you have to keep tending and adjusting and making improvements once I'm gone. No matter how successful you get, you cannot slack off or the grass is going to grow, the paint is going to peel, and the roads will start to crumble. Stop hustling, and everything you learn here will be useless. Your success is entirely up to you.

turn water into wine

Here's the deal: if you want it badly enough, the money is there, the success is there, and the fulfillment is there. All you have to do is take it. So quit whining, quit crying, quit with the excuses. If you already have a full-time job, you can get a lot done between 7:00 P.M. and 2:00 A.M. (9:00 P.M. to 3:00 A.M. if you've got kids), so learn to love working during those predawn hours. I promise it won't be hard if you're doing what you love more than anything else. I don't care if your passion is rehabilitating abandoned ferrets; if you learn to tap into everything the digital world has to offer, you can turn water into wine—you can transform what you love into a legacy-building business that makes a crapload of money, and still be true to yourself.

Ultimately this book is not about making a million dollars, although it just might help you do that. It's about ensuring your own happiness by enabling you to live every day passionately and productively. Business is not just about making money, and if you think it is, you're broken. If you're already familiar with the social marketing tools we'll discuss in this book, I hope you'll pay attention to the big picture. It's too easy to forget what really matters once you're digging deep in these trenches.

Learn to navigate the digital waters of social marketing to build a business and promote a personal brand based around what you love most, and you will only be limited by how far you want to sail. Social media tools—Facebook, Twitter, Flickr, and all the rest—are modern-day galleons that will carry you to the new world, allowing you to share your passion, differentiate yourself from your competitors, and deliver your brand to the broadest possible audience.

My secret to success is just one guy's way of doing things, of course, but do things my way—adapted to what works for your DNA, of course—and total happiness is yours.

two

---

success is in your dna

am a walking contradiction. No one believes in himself more than I do, yet I'm well aware of how unimportant I really am. I couldn't care less what people think about me, but I do respect and pay attention to what they say. When viewers posted comments on a recent episode of Diggnation (one of the biggest video blogs on the Internet) saying that I was obnoxious in the forums of the show, I stayed up until 4:00 A.M. apologizing to every one of them. I love building businesses and launching new ventures, but the only reason I value money is that I'm going to need a lot of it when I buy the New York Jets (I'm not kidding, I really do want to own the Jets! This has been an obsession of mine since third grade). And although the story of how I became what *ABC News* called the "Social Media Sommelier," Slate referred to as "the wine guru for the YouTube era," and *Nightline* named "the Wayne's World wine aficionado" is in some ways the most common immigrant-makes-good story ever told, it's also unheard of, not only because the technology that made it possible didn't exist until a few years ago but because no one else has my DNA.

For a business guy, I talk a lot about DNA, and this book will be no exception. That's because I firmly believe that the path to your successful business literally lies in the twists and turns of your own double helix. In fact, I should probably just credit the success of Wine Library TV, the online wine-tasting video blog that put me on the social marketing map, to my mom and dad, who gave me the DNA that enabled me to take my career to a thunderous level. Then again, lots of ambitious people have been born with great DNA and yet eventually found themselves at a professional standstill, frustrated, miserable, stuck. Why? Because they weren't doing what they loved more than anything else in the world; they weren't doing what they were born to do.

you gotta be you

I got lucky. From a very early age I knew and accepted the dictates of my DNA, which were that I was born to be a people person and to build businesses. Those were and have always been my passions. I knew I was made to be an entrepreneur and not once did I try to be anything else, as evidenced by the D- and F-infested report cards I'd bring home that gave my mother conniptions. Even though I hated to make my mother cry, I also knew that I had to be me, and if that meant hiding the *Beckett Baseball Guide* inside my math book during class so I could read up for my next baseball card trading show, that's the way it had to be. Too many people ignore their DNA, however, to conform to what their families or society expects of them. A lot of people also decide that professional success has to look a certain way. That's how someone born to design bikes winds up becoming a lawyer, or someone who loves experimenting with makeup works every day pitching someone else's overpriced brand to malls around the country, or someone who cannot go a day without jotting down some ideas for their next poem spends most of their time at the helm of an emergency IT department. To me that's insane.

I've been dying to do this book, not because I think I can help everyone who wants to become a millionaire—although I'm pretty sure I can—but because it drives me crazy to know that there are still people out there who haven't figured out that they don't have to settle. There is no excuse for anyone living in the United States or anywhere else right now to slog through his or her entire life working at jobs they hate, or even jobs they simply don't love, in the name of a paycheck or a sense of responsibility. The Internet makes it possible for anyone to be 100 percent true to themselves and make serious cash by turning what they love most into their personal brand. There no longer has to be a difference between who you are and what you do.

Now, as cuddly and cozy as this follow-your-bliss message might seem, make no mistake—if you do things the way I tell you to do them, you're going to work harder than you've ever worked in your life. But I'm of the opinion that hardship shapes us. Coming from nothing served my family well. It also gave me the hunger to want it all, and the wisdom to know that none of it matters. I'm convinced, in fact, that if things had been a little easier for my family in the early days, I never would have gotten to where I am now. To tell that story, we have to go back to the Old Country.

coming to america

My family moved here from Belarus, in the former Soviet Union, in 1978. My father, Sasha, was inspired to come to the States by a great-uncle who had emigrated years before. He came back to Belarus to visit his sister and that's how my father learned that America was a place where you could build a life for yourself according to your own rules, and you didn't have to wait six hours in line to buy a loaf of bread, either. A natural entrepreneur, my father knew that America was where his family's future lay. As Jews we were given special permission to seek political asylum abroad, and after months of working through red tape and cooling our heels in Austria and Italy, we finally landed in Queens, New York. Unfortunately, my great-uncle died unexpectedly right before our journey began, yet his children were kind to us—Mom, Dad, three-year-old me (then named Gennady), my grandmother, and my great-grandparents—until we could move into a studio apartment arranged by a Jewish foundation. We arrived certain that the streets were paved with proverbial gold.

Grandma got mugged within about six weeks. The economy was tanking, and the construction job my dad had arranged before arriving to this country evaporated within a few months. Again my great-uncle's family helped out by offering my dad a job as a stock boy in one of their liquor stores in Clark, New Jersey.

Times were tough. I still get emotional when I think about the time my parents walked a few miles to and from Kmart to buy me not one, but two *Star Wars* action figures for my sixth birthday. For families on a tight budget like us—my sister, Elizabeth, was born by then—that was a big deal. I don't remember anyone complaining much about money, though, or about anything else for that matter. We had our health and we had one another, what more did we need?

We assimilated quickly—my parents changed my name to Gary when we arrived—but inside the home, it was still Belarus. No way was my mother plopping meat loaf down for dinner like those American moms. In our house we ate stuffed cabbage and smoked herring. We never took medicine, only tea; and if you were really sick, you rubbed vodka on your chest. I never wanted to tell anyone I had gotten a cut or burn on my hand because they would immediately suggest I pee on it.

My dad was smart and he knew how to hustle, so it didn't take long for him to work his way up and become manager, then co-owner of the small liquor store in Clark. By 1983, he had bought a store the size of an office with a partner in Springfield, and later he built that same store up to four thousand square feet. Years later, after I got involved in the business, we built the current Wine Library on the same property. It's forty thousand square feet, a far cry from the original store, which was called Shopper's Discount Liquors and looked exactly what you would think a Shopper's Discount Liquors should look like.

My parents were hungry—hungry to provide for their family, and hungry to win. My dad worked his ass off, so much that I really didn't get to know him until I was fourteen years old. Yet I have tremendous respect for what he did for us. Thanks to his hard work and chutzpah, we became the epitome of the American success story. In 1978, we were broke and couldn't speak English; in 1985, I was the first kid on my block to have Nintendo. You can see why my dad is my hero. My gratitude for what he did drives my own ambition to take my business to higher and higher levels.

rise of the entrepreneur

On the surface my dad and I are very different, though I have a lot of his fire and hustle. I'm a lot like my mom, superemotional, and a true people person, open to everyone from day one but very strong on the inside. Dad is a tougher guy to get close to. He is slower to let you in, but once he does, you are family. I respect him to no end, but I wish more people could get to know him. The other big difference between us is that he allows his emotions to lead his decisions. I am all about passion, but letting your emotional trigger finger make your business calls is a big no-no in my book.

Observing me from an early age, however, no one could deny that my dad's entrepreneurial DNA ran strong through me. The only thing I loved more than running a business and making money was the New York Jets. My neighbor always said that no season was safe. In the summer I would wash her car, in the fall I'd rake her leaves, and I'd shovel her snow through the winter. There was one spring when I cut the flowers in her yard, then rang her doorbell and sold a bouquet back to her. I'm still kind of proud of that initiative; the profit margin was amazing.

By the time I was eight years old, I had seven lemonade stands and was raking in crazy amounts of cash for someone who was still too scared to ride a bike. My fear was problematic consid-

ering that my franchises were located all around the neighborhood. Everyone could hear me coming from a mile away as I
roared around on my Big Wheel to pick up my money.

My real business education began when I caught baseball
fever. My mom had taken me to a flea market, where I bought
some packs of baseball cards as well as a copy of the *Beckett
Baseball Card Price Guide*. It revealed that there was actual value
to the cards I had bought. I can still remember the feeling as
I realized that my world was changed. It was the same feeling
I'd get later when I saw the market potential for wine, when I
saw the Internet for the first time, and when I watched the first
video blog. Game over. Good-bye lemonade stands, hello baseball cards. We moved to Hunterdon County, New Jersey, when I
was in eighth grade. Baseball cards were on like Donkey Kong at
my new school, and within weeks I was raking in the dough.

One day the local mall personnel announced they were hosting a baseball card show, and no way was I going to miss it. I was
already a hundred-dollar player thanks to selling cards to my
eighth-grade classmates, so I mustered up my courage and asked
my dad for the biggest number I could think of—a thousand dollars. Unbelievably (though in hindsight that's just who my dad
is), he gave it to me. The money was burning a hole in my pocket,
so I immediately went to Costco and spent it on several boxes of
cards. I knew they weren't a good year but I was impatient (the
last time I would ever be that). Sure enough, when I opened them
and looked up their value in the price guide I found out they
were worth only about two hundred dollars. Oh, man, I was in
trouble.

My mom drove my two partners, Jason Riker and John Churcak, and me to the mall so we could buy a table at the show. We had agreed ahead of time that we wouldn't buy a table if it cost more than twenty bucks. We asked for the promoter, and this four-hundred-pound Italian dude comes out. "Hey mister," I said, "how much for the show?" A hundred and fifty bucks. $150! I handed over the money, shook the guy's hand, and walked away, ignoring my friends' gaping mouths. My brain was telling me this was a terrible idea, but my gut said, "Go for it," and I've always listened to my gut.

By the time I got home and told my dad and mom what I had done I was almost in tears, but true to form, they didn't throttle me, even though I'm sure they wanted to. Instead, my dad said he hoped that losing the money would be worth the experience. He's a wise man, my dad. I went to my room determined to show him that I wasn't in this just for the experience. The fire was burning, and there was no way I was going to lose.

The next day we set up our table and the first thing I did was market research—I walked around the show checking out what everyone else was selling. I then adjusted, repricing every card we had that was available for less than anyone else was selling it. We crushed it and made straight cash. From then on, I did every show I could. My mom and fellow card dealer and best friend Brandon Warnke's mom would drive us in the snow or rain to Bridgewater, Hillsborough, Edison, Raritan, anywhere there was a show, and every time I'd dominate. I had just learned one of my first lessons in business—scarcity breeds desire. My strategy was simple, I'd buy sets that weren't mentioned in *Beckett*'s and promote them to create a market. You're thinking, jeez, Gary, what a scam artist you were. Not at all. I was an optimist. A pessimist would have seen the cards were unlisted and assumed they were worthless. I, on the other hand, quite innocently decided that if these cards weren't in the guide, they had to be valuable.

I paid my dad back his thousand dollars in about three or four months, and I continued to earn that kind of money every weekend I could. Then I turned fifteen and got dragged out of the mall and into the liquor store.

learning the trade

To go from self-made baseball card king of Hunterdon County rolling in the dough to grunt bagging ice for two bucks an hour was a hard fall. It wasn't until I turned sixteen that I was even allowed up on the floor and became a cashier. Not too exciting, but it beat hours of shoveling ice and dusting shelves. I couldn't drink anything we sold (my parents were strict about that), but I was good at regurgitating data, so when business was slow I'd flip through trade magazines to pass the time and then use what I'd learned to help customers. One of those magazines was *Wine Spectator*. Now, the store was called Shopper's Discount Liquors for a reason. Most of our business came from selling the hard stuff. Beer, too, was a big seller—the beer cooler took up about 33 percent of the entire store. But I learned two things from my time behind the cash register. First, thanks to *Wine Spectator,* I learned that there was a whole cultural cachet to drinking wine and that people collected it the same way I collected baseball cards, *Star Wars* toys, and comic books. That was interesting to me. I also started noticing a pattern: people would come in to buy their Absolut or their Johnnie Walker and I knew that I or any staff could talk until we were blue in the face about the other brands, they were still walking out with their Absolut or their Johnnie Walker. Those brands were just too established. The wine buyer, though, would often walk in looking a little lost and spend ten minutes tentatively peering at labels as though hoping a bottle would jump out and spare them from making a decision. I knew from my experience with the baseball card business that people want to be told what's good and valuable, and that they enjoy feeling like they've been turned on to something not everyone can appreciate.

Storytelling is by far the most underrated skill in business.

The wine buyers, unlike the liquor customers, were open to any suggestions I had, and I realized that they represented opportunity. Spotting that social trend was enough to turn what started out as a casual interest in wine into an obsession. I had started out at Shopper's Discount Liquors hating every second of my time there, but now I was determined to turn the place into the number one wine shop in America.

changing the wine world

No one had any illusions that I was a great scholar as I started my senior year of high school, so it made sense to me that my plan should be to eke out the grades to graduate and start working full-time at the liquor store. Some time in February . . . yes, February (sorry, Mom, you know it's true) . . . my mother asked me what college I was planning to attend. College? As luck would have it, a postcard from Mount Ida College in Newton, Massachusetts, showed up in the mail a few days later. I filled it out, and Mount Ida became my home in the fall. By then, though, my life was the store, and I'd come home almost every weekend to work there.

In September 1995, I was hanging out in a friend's dorm room when he turned on his computer and introduced me to this thing called the Internet. I let my friends bumble around chat rooms trying to meet girls for a little while, then kicked them off and spent the next nine hours hunting down baseball card trading forums and figuring out how I was going to use this thing to grow the store. There was no doubt in my mind this was going to be the future of business. It would take me another year to get the courage to approach my dad about selling wine online. What can I say, my dad was a scary guy. At first he resisted. But he believed in me, and as soon as he relented I was off to the races.

Winelibrary.com launched in June 1997 (the store itself wouldn't take on the name Wine Library until 1999). The store brought in about 2 or 3 million per year in 1994. I came onboard full-time after graduating in 1998 and grew the business from about 4 million to 10 million in a year with 0 percent of that in online sales. By 2001, we were doing about 20 million. Not bad. Not bad at all. Life was good and business was booming. Most guys my age would have thought they had it made.

Then, on my thirtieth birthday, November 14, 2005, I was driving along the New Jersey Turnpike on my way to work thinking about my day, and I realized that as perfect as life seemed, I wasn't entirely happy. I knew deep in my soul that there was no way I was ever going to buy the Jets if I stayed on the retail path. It was time to go big.

We had a computer department at Wine Library by now, and I had seen Erik Kastner and John Kassimatis spending their lunch breaks spitting food all over themselves from laughing at these things called video blogs (the two big ones at the time were *Rocketboom* and *the show with zefrank*). I had been trying to figure out how to leverage this new medium to show people that there was more to drink out there than Yellowtail. I'd also noticed that sites like MySpace and Flickr and YouTube were becoming popular, sites that had nothing to do with commerce and everything to do with being social and sharing stories and meeting people, and that was something I was good at. It was there, on the New Jersey Turnpike, that I had my *aha* moment. I wasn't going to use video blogs to sell wine; I was going to use video blogs to build a whole new world for wine, and for myself. I waited to get the store through the holiday season, and then launched Wine Library TV in February 2006, three months later.

three

build your personal brand

You've just read a piece of my story that most people don't know, and it's probably the most important part. I'll say it again: Wine Library TV was never about selling wine on the Internet. It was always about building brand equity.

Some people might point out that if I weren't interested in selling wine, I wouldn't include links to buy it on the Wine Library TV site. Believe me, I'd make more money doing an affiliate program with Wine.com than I do with my links to Winelibrary.com. But I'm a businessman—if someone wants to buy wine from me, be my guest. However, so that no one can accuse "The Thunder Show" (my nickname for Wine Library TV) of being an extended sales pitch, I make sure that Wine Library only carries fifteen or fewer cases of whatever I talk about. If I give something a good review and it sells out, everyone has to go elsewhere to get it. If the goal of Wine Library TV were to sell wine, I'd make sure to have enough product on hand to serve my customers. Wine Library, our store, doesn't reap commercial benefits from Wine Library TV because of an uptick in sales due to my blog; it reaps brand equity benefits because people come to the store to see what it's about and where I work. Sometimes they just come to thank me for the content on my blog, which I really, really appreciate.

Developing your personal brand is key to monetizing your passion online. Whether you're delivering your content by video, podcast, or blog, it's the authentic you, the one thing that is guaranteed to differentiate you from everybody else, including those who share your niche or business model. The thing that most people don't realize is that in today's world your business and your personal brand need to be one and the same, whether you're selling organic fish food or financial advice or just your opinion.

Monetizing a personal brand is not a new concept. A lot of the most successful entertainment figures in the world are personal brand geniuses, like Oprah, Howard Stern, and Emeril. They built their empires out of being who they are and never backing down from it. But the major benefits of personal branding are not limited to the A-list celebrities. In fact, personal branding is what gives everyone an unprecedented shot at joining their ranks. For example, think about what some people might consider second-tier celebrities like Ashton Kutcher or Kerry Rhodes. Kutcher was already famous from his stints on television, not to mention his marriage to Demi Moore, but there is no doubt that his brand has blown up since he started leveraging social networking tools. Rhodes, the New York Jets football player, has been using Twitter with incredible success to make his brand bigger. D-to-C-level entertainment figures like Will Wheaton, Brooke Burke, Levar Burton, and Fred Durst are building great opportunities that will likely propel them from B- to A-level status. How do I know? Because I can see how many people are following them on their Twitter accounts. Now, usually I advise people to ignore the quantity of people following them and focus instead on the quality of their interactions with those followers—it's a lot more indicative of how well their brand is doing. Many decision makers, however, still aren't aware of this important detail, and therefore the preceding celebrities will benefit from those nice numbers we're seeing. Where the eyeballs go, opportunity follows.

Last, but by no means least, are the people whom you might have never heard of who are putting out great content and leveraging social media and killing it, like Dave Morin @davemorin, Chris Sacca @sacca, Justine Ezarik @ijustine, and Kevin Rose @kevinrose. Their personal brands are skyrocketing, and there's no reason to think that eventually they won't become household names.

You see where I'm going with this? The first generation built their brands on television and movie screens, radio, magazines, and newspapers, and the new one will do the same online at a much lower cost, with no need for a gatekeeper's approval. Get into position, because the big killing is coming around the corner. The field may be different, but the game is just the same.

building my brand

If you watch me on Winelibrarytv.com, you'll figure out my personal brand pretty quickly. I'm the wine guy who tells it like it is in plain English. It's a brand that I've been able to develop from a very early age, thanks to growing up in the wine industry. I'd attend $1,000-a-head tastings and rub elbows with experienced connoisseurs who had lived a long time in the wine trenches. This meant that they had lots of expertise to share with a relative newcomer like me. It also meant that they carried a load of baggage in the form of preconceived notions of how things should be.

They'd swirl and smell and slurp and spit and then spout the same classic terminology every time, how the bouquet was rose petals or the finish was silk. I would stick my nose in my glass, suck in a mouthful of air and wine, and the only thing running through my head would be, "Man, this really tastes like Big League Chew," or, "If this isn't a Whatchamacallit bar, I don't know what is." It's not that I couldn't spout an A-to-Z wine-tasting lexicon and didn't appreciate the complexity of an excellent vintage. I knew my Malbec from my Montepulciano; I just didn't see why I had to use the same forty-five-cent words to describe my experience when drinking it. On top of that, everyone, including the reviewers, was drinking and admiring the same damn stuff. If Cloudy Bay Sauvignon Blanc were featured as the best white of 1998, we'd see a surge in demand for it at the store. Never mind that as far as I was concerned the Babich was a million times better and a better deal since it cost about half the price.

It was clear to me that the industry was stuck in a rut, and my experience in the store told me that people were dying for someone to take the mystery out of wine buying and make it fun. And I thought, this I can do. So I became the wine guy, and that's how I built my personal brand, not with wine per se. I offer my personal brand, not wine, on Wine Library TV. Every episode gives me a chance to share my considerable expertise with other people interested in the same thing I am, which is loads of fun. They also give me a chance to share myself. Watch me for two seconds and you know exactly who I am and what I stand for. Authenticity is key.

Now, that can definitely be a double-edged sword. I know there are people out there who think I'm a jerk with my Jets spit bucket, my table littered with toys, and my colorful language. I'm loud, I'm over the top, I'm hyper. But I am who I am. I'm for real, and overall people like that. People watch, and they listen, and they even learn a thing or two and sometimes agree with me that hell yes, this Reisling does taste like a racquetball. I give wine lovers the permission to like any kind of wine they like, whether it's White Zinfandel or serious Bordeaux.

I cultivated another brand too, of course, the one that got me this book deal and the keynote speeches and the consulting gigs, as well as helped me and my brother, AJ, build VaynerMedia. For almost two years I was patient. I let people get to know me and trust my wine guy personal brand. Then in October 2007, I decided I needed to scratch my itch. The world was ready to know that I was more than the funny guy who knows a lot about wine. I woke up one morning and thought, *It's time to talk biz,* and I started airing videos of me talking about my real passion, building brands and business.

Regardless of which brand people are drawn to, my popularity stems from the fact that I know what the hell I'm talking about, and that I'm honest. For all my charisma and entertainment value, if the content I was putting out wasn't any good and couldn't be trusted, no one would be watching. No one.

To everyone who is freaking out because they fear the noise and distraction of all the additional content on the Internet, you can relax. Quality is a tremendous filter. Cream always rises, my friends, no matter how many cups of coffee you pour.

---

opportunity lies in transparency

Consumers want you to tell them the truth. Sure, they want quality and service and value and entertainment, but above all they want to know that the person they're dealing with is being honest. Entrepreneurs don't really have a choice—the lines between the private and the public are becoming increasingly blurred, and with people able to share their experiences and thoughts and photographs on video by spraying them all over the Internet within minutes after they happen, the days of being able to con the consumer without repercussions are pretty much over. So no matter how you shape and color your personal brand, honesty has got to be at your core.

I come online five days a week to taste and review wines. Some wines are tremendous, some taste like horse crap. Do the makers of the wines I pan like me? Probably not. Do I care? Nope. Do I sell some of the ones that I think taste bad? You bet I do, because you might totally disagree with me (someone at the winery who made them sure did). All I'm doing on my blog is being myself and voicing my opinion loud and clear. When you launch your videos, blogs, or podcasts, you're going to do the same. That goes for everyone, including those of you who are used to keeping information close to the vest, or you will lose, one way or another.

Let's say you're in real estate and you love it. Part of the real-estate game is learning to put some serious spin on a loser property, right? You pitch it as a "charming fixer-upper" or a gem "just waiting for some TLC." Even the appealing properties get the rose-colored treatment. But what if you sat down in front of a camera and posted a series of video blogs telling people what you really thought of the homes or commercial sites or lots you were selling? What if you said something like, "I have got one ugly house to sell. Seriously, folks, you've got to see this one if only to take in one of the last surviving examples of red shag carpeting matched with faux-deer-antler, woodland-creature chandeliers. The sellers are supernice and I would love to get them the $360K they originally wanted, but I've talked to them about it and they understand that they need to set their sights lower because this sucker needs some serious renovations. I'm thinking you should take a look at it if you've got about $275K to spend, plus some extra bucks for a contractor. And bring your imagination. Lots of it."

Now, I know there are laws in real estate that might make it hard to execute this idea. Clearly, I was pushing the limits in the last paragraph. But would that kind of transparency hurt your business? Maybe at first you'd have a hard time getting sellers to list with you. But imagine what kind of coin you'd earn if you became the most trusted real-estate agent in town because no one would ever doubt that you'd try to sell them a house you didn't think was worth every dime for which you were asking? Your listings would go up because sellers would be confident their properties weren't going to gather dust on the market, your sales would go up because buyers would know they weren't going to have to deal with any bs. On top of that, you'd have the satisfaction of doing something you loved entirely your way. And on top of *that*, you'd have built a solid personal brand—the no-bs real-estate agent—that you can now carry with you wherever you go and use as leverage to find bigger and better professional opportunities, including book-writing gigs, television appearances, and a variety of other media appearances.

Do it. Do it right now.

One real-estate agent who is building a powerful online personal brand is Ian Watt at www.ianwatt.ca. Every video blog he launches as he drives around the streets of Vancouver, where he's based, dispenses Ian's thoughts on the real-estate business and the state of the market or offers general advice to property buyers and sellers. He's lively, he's knowledgeable, and he's crushing it big-time.

---

trust your own palate

When you're thinking about your personal brand, don't worry that it will have to look anything like mine in order for you to crush it. You'll crush it as long as you concentrate on being yourself. Besides, you can't be like me. I like wines that you don't. I like White Castle and the New York Knicks, and you probably don't. I'd rather drink a V8 than any fruit juice, and I hoover my veggies. All of those quirks and preferences have shaped my brand. Your brand will be unique and interesting because you are unique and interesting. Don't put on an act to try to imitate me or anyone else who's had some success with social marketing. You will lose because people can sniff out a poser from a mile away. I had to wait a long time to find a platform that allowed me to create and share an authentic personal brand. Before I launched Wine Library TV, I saw that blogs were on the rise and I knew there was opportunity there and was desperate to get in on it. But I looked in the mirror and asked, "Can you write? No . . . Damn!"* Now, I could have hired someone to write elegant blog posts for me and pretended they were mine (note to some celebrities I won't name: I love you but cut that out, we know you're not writing those tweets on Twitter yourself), but I knew that if I was going to get people interested in me, everything was going to have to come straight from me, unfiltered and unpolished. Creating and disseminating my content would be the only thing that I absolutely could not and would not delegate. Besides, if I was going to spend the time building a gazillion-dollar business so that I could buy the Jets, I had to do it in a way that was authentically me and that I couldn't wait to do every day. So I waited until I found a medium that spoke to my DNA—video blogs—jumped on it, and never looked back.

Embrace your DNA, be yourself, put out awesome content,

---

*Remember what I said in chapter 1 about partnering with someone whose DNA complements yours? To do this book, I teamed up with someone who does know how to write, and I dictated the whole thing.

and people will be interested in what you have to say. Believe me, if you're that good, people are going to find you, and they're going to follow you, and they're going to talk. And getting people to talk is the whole point.

word of mouth on steroids

Leveraging social networking platforms into effective conduits for your personal brand is all about building word of mouth. There's nothing new in that. Since the first six handfuls of grain were handed over in exchange for a new ox, business owners have always known that what their customers and their friends, family, or colleagues think about their restaurant or car or vacation spot or cleaning service or design firm has always mattered more than any billboard or radio ad they could buy. But there have always been a finite number of people their customers and friends, family, or colleagues could talk to about their experience with their products or services.

Now, though, the Internet and social networks—and the instant access to online communities (and the millions of people who will eventually join them) they provide—have pumped word of mouth up like it was on steroids. The consumer is no longer limited to talking about her experience with your personal brand to the people in her immediate circle or even in random encounters during her day. Now, if she's got a Twitter account, she can tell five thousand people that she just read your hilarious blog post about breeding Siamese cats. And since those aren't just five thousand random people, they're five thousand people who have deliberately told your Twitter reader they want to hear what she thinks, chances are superb that a good percentage of them are going to be curious enough to check out your blog for themselves. And like in a brick-and-mortar business, half the battle is getting them in the door. If they like you, many will turn right around and repost your reader's comment to all of the people following them. And so on and so forth. Now, how long did it take you, the Siamese cat breeder, to reach thousands upon thousands of potential blog readers and customers this way, for free no less? Ten minutes, give or take. It's mind-blowing, and every day more and more tools are being created to carry your personal brand further.

everybody's doing it

You may not have started your business yet, but there's a good chance you've already created a personal brand without even re-alizing it. You become one the second you create any kind of Internet account that puts you in the public eye. Facebook, My-Space, Twitter—social networking sites, yes, but personal brand-ing sites, too. Don't think so? Let's say you're a shutterbug and you use your Facebook or Flickr account to post your best pho-tographs. You've just made it possible for someone whose pas-sion is business development with expertise in advertising to see them. Next thing you know, you get an e-mail asking if you want to earn cash by shooting stock photos in your area. I know this might sound pie-in-the-sky, but it happens every day. I've seen it with my own eyes. You have to understand that we're living in a world where word of mouth is allowing content to travel faster and further than ever before. It's passed around and around until finally it falls into the right hands. I'm telling you, once you join the digital world you're in play, so you'd better be prepared.

Maybe you think that you have no need to create a personal brand because you like your job or you work for a corporation. What, you think you're invincible? Even if the economy were soaring, I would be telling you to start using social media tools to share your ideas with the world and make yourself a recognizable brand. What if you're a trader at an investment firm and suddenly you're out of work and all you have to show is a bull-crap résumé? *Hold it,* you might want to reassure me, *my résumé is awesome.* Tell me this: Is it a pdf of a tidy list of where you've worked and for how long, with a couple of strategic bullet points highlighting what you did in each job? Yeah? You're toast. Keep your pdf so that the HR department has something for their files, but otherwise traditional résumés are going to be irrelevant, and soon. Even if they're not yet, that résumé you're so proud of looks exactly like the ones being waved around by the other three hundred analysts in your city currently hunting for jobs.

Developing your personal brand is the same thing as living and breathing your résumé every second that you're working. Your latest tweet and comment on Facebook and most recent blog post? That's your résumé now. That's how you are going to announce to the world your ideas and opinions, the very things that make you unique and reveal why a firm—or better yet, a passionate entrepreneur cherry-picking top talent to build a whole new kind of investment company—would be dumb not to hire you. Think about how different your situation would look if you got laid off but had been keeping up your personal brand and become well established as a hot commodity. Before, it would have taken hours of phone calls and e-mails to announce you were available. Today, thirty minutes after getting the bad news you'd write a blog post, then send out a tweet and a status update on Facebook about your situation, and immediately every manager in the industry would know you were looking for a job and, since they'd already be familiar with your brand, think, *Hmm, how can I get her onboard here?*

It's a fact that hiring decisions are made every day because of personal connections. If you're a sales manager at Crest, every post you make online could have an agenda, whether it's to reveal your thoughts on your industry—"We've got to come up with a fresh approach to packaging"—or to reveal your thoughts in general—"I think I want to take up ice hockey." You cannot afford to be one-dimensional; everything you say that you think is irrelevant is now relevant. Think of all that online commentary you post as your half of one long, friendly lunch interview. If a manager is hiring and has the choice between two equally qualified candidates, she's going to choose the one with whom she's experienced some kind of bond, whether it's a mutual belief in revamping the toothpaste industry or a shared love for ice hockey. Through your content you're making sure that people can get to know you personally and professionally. Now, because your personal brand is already well known and respected, if you need a job and there is a position that needs to be filled, you'll likely be the first one called. If you've built your brand right, those established firms will be out of luck because the biz dev guy who has been following you—someone like me—will have already invited you to participate in an exciting new venture. Your days of working to put money in someone else's pockets are over.

four

a whole new world

Business in the future is going to be a field day for everyone with talent because they'll no longer be forced to exist within the confines of old-guard institutions. For example, everyone who is screaming that journalism is dead because newspapers and magazines are folding is insane. The old platforms are in trouble, but that's the best thing that could happen to journalists . . . the good ones, anyway.

The platforms are sinking because the readers are going online, which means that the ad money is going online. So of course journalists should go online, too. But their opportunity is not as a work-for-hire, where they scramble to earn a few bucks here, a few bucks there writing pieces for various online publications, nor as a staff writer earning pennies while the company keeps a disproportionate amount of the ad revenue brought in on the backs of poorly paid talent.

Unlike people in most fields, journalists are constantly building brand equity through their work. So all talented journalists have to do is take advantage of the technological and cultural shifts that are sinking their media platforms like leaky ships, go into business for themselves, and crush it. I make it sound so easy, right? I know it's not. But guess what? It's the future, and those journalists and reporters who get wise to that truth are the ones who are going to survive.

Now, some reporters and journalists are probably not business savvy enough to launch a new business on their own, though those who possess that rare combination of fiery entrepreneurial spirit and reporting chops could team up and form a killer online news service without any biz dev partnership at all. They're going to win really big. But journalists with less business sense but massive talent won't be left out in the cold. I guarantee that as more business developers recognize the huge potential in this market, they are going to start recruiting top talent to join them in new ventures.

What might these ventures look like? We've already seen that small, lean, tight business models—like Politico.com, realclearpolitics.com, seekingalpha.com, and minyanville.com—can work. The new generation of online news is going to be more democratic. Maybe we'll see a four-person journalist staff team up with a fifth business partner to create thedailyscoop.com. Everyone owns a 20 percent stake in the company (obviously you can have a forty-person team and everyone would just own fewer points). They won't report breaking news at first (and let's be honest, how much of what you read in the paper these days broke the day before online or on TV?). Rather, they'll focus on using social media to pump out provocative analysis. They do that for a year and build up cash flow through advertising, which would stream in because as we all know, money follows eyeballs, and these guys are good enough to draw a lot of viewers. With enough revenue in place they would eventually be able to hire more great journalists and launch investigative reporting. These reporters won't get paid $80,000 to go to Afghanistan, they'll get paid a 7 percent equity of a "thirteen-million-dollar-per-year" business that's only going to grow and grow, and some of the reporting from Afghanistan will come from someone local armed with a combination cell phone/Flip Cam (they're coming, you watch) who streams the news live.

There are lots of other ways these new businesses could play out. What's to stop the ten most popular journalists at the *Wall Street Journal* from banding together in conjunction with a business partner to create their own online all-star team? Or maybe they could launch an online newspaper in which every time an article gets a click-through, the journalist who wrote it gets two bucks. Sure, there will be writers who might try to game the system and ethical questions will inevitably come up, but anyone who goes down that path is going to get exposed, guaranteed. There have always been people in every industry with hidden agendas, but now there is no place for them to hide.

News is also going to get more local, and we're going to see news paparazzi. There will be a personal brand called The News Maverick, a newer version of Geraldo Rivera, who becomes known for jumping fences with his cell phone/Flip Cam and breaking major stories. What will that be worth? Plenty.

News has been functioning under a communistic regime, but capitalism always wins. Critics can argue with me and say that these new models demean the training and insight and education it takes to be a great journalist, and perhaps that's true, but crying about how things should be instead of embracing how things are doesn't do anyone any good. The changes affecting the news business are permanent. Fundamental supply and demand is shifting. Quantity is up, price is down, which means the cost structure has to shrink dramatically. And like it or not, many people's respect for quality reporting has eroded. This upsets me as much as the next guy, but the fact is that it's a trend that is having a huge impact on business and needs to be noticed and accepted. To explore and analyze all the sides of this story with the depth it deserves would unfortunately require way more space than this book allows, but I assure you, this is how things are going to roll. The only arguments I get in this debate, by the way, are from journalists and individuals with an emotional attachment to the idea of ink on paper and the romance of sipping a cup of coffee while reading the Sunday *Times*. Most businesspeople know I'm right.

If the traditional platforms are sinking ships, then journalists are sailors who need to jump. If they're not strong enough to get to the new ship, yes, they're going to drown. But those who are great swimmers are going to sail very, very far. That is the way business has always played and always will. It's a truth at the heart of this book—the game is changing, and your opportunity is huge if you take it.

The middleman has not yet been eliminated, but we're getting there. A lot has been made of how the music and news industries have been turned upside down by Internet technology, but anyone who thinks the revolution is going to stop there is naive. The massive sea change that is rocking the news industry is going to rock every industry that relies on human interaction. And can you think of any business that isn't in some way dependent on human interaction? I can't. The changes that will be wrought by the Internet are as fundamentally transformative to content and commerce as the printing press. It's a whole new world; build your personal brand and get ready for it.

plan your future now

If you don't plan ahead and decide where you want to go, you're in big trouble. My feeling is that no matter how much you like your job, you should aim to leave it and grow your own brand and business or partner with someone to do so, because as long as you're working for someone else you will never be living entirely true to yourself and your passion. That said, I will never tell anyone to quit their job, especially if they've got other people to support. Family first, remember. I will, however, tell you to start planning to quit your job if you can't answer yes to the following checklist:

1. Are you happy with your present job? Like, really happy. Like you don't bitch and moan every Monday morning about how much you wish it were Friday night.
2. Do you work for a company that allows you to have a public persona, either about your field or your true passion (which when I'm through I'll have convinced you should be one and the same, but I'll cut you some slack for now)? In other words, are you allowed to have a blog,

a Twitter account, or otherwise brand yourself in the public eye with an identity that is separate from that of the corporation? Some industries, like finance and law, will not allow this. If your passion is finance or law, do you love your field enough to make that sacrifice? Do you think you'll love it as much in ten or twenty years and not regret missing out on all the opportunities inherent in social media?

3. If you're not allowed to develop a public persona at work, are you allowed to do so during your personal time?

If you answer no to numbers 2 and 3, I don't care how happy you are now, you should do everything you can to find another place to work or start the groundwork to launch your own business, because eventually you are going to suffocate. Any company that clamps down on its best talent and doesn't allow them to talk to the public is holding that talent back from where the business world is going, and you don't want to be left behind. Without the freedom to develop a personal brand, you will find yourself at a strong disadvantage to the competition that will have been pumping out that content and making a name for themselves.

If you're not happy in your job but you can still build brand equity at work or at home by blogging or creating podcasts about what you love, I still want you to plan to leave and launch your own business because life is way too short to spend it working in a job you don't love. I'm not as worried about you, though, as I am about someone who's happy but not allowed to talk to the public, because as long as you're creating content and building your brand you're building future opportunity.

But if you're not happy at work, and faceless, and have been forbidden to talk about your passion to the world, get the hell out as soon as you can. You've got no chance otherwise of creating a personal brand, and without one, you're professionally dead in the water.

Look, financial security is important, but if you love sneakers and you know more about them and are more passionate about them than anyone else on earth, you can make money talking about them. I believe that with every ounce of my soul.

Recently Tara Swiger announced she was quitting her day job to devote herself entirely to Blondechickenboutique.com, where she is building a passionate community of fiber growers and artisans; she sells hand-dyed organic yarn and blogs about knitting, dyeing, and other domestic arts. She's clearly crushing it. Why can't you?

---

five

create great content

To monetize your personal brand into a business using social marketing networks, two pillars need to be in place: product and content.

We've talked about how to choose your product, which should be whatever you're most passionate about. Whatever it is, it should go without saying that quality counts in a major way. You can hustle and market and network all you want, but if your sports drink tastes like trash, or if you're putting out bad information, you're going to lose.

know your stuff

Great content is what you're going to pump into your social media networks to draw eyeballs to your blog. It exists as a result of passion plus expertise, so make sure you can talk about your product like no one else. Do your homework. You should be reading and absorbing every single resource you can find—books, trade journals, newsletters, websites, as well as taking classes and attending lectures and conferences (you're also going to visit and interact with other people's blogs on the same subject, but there's a method to that, which we'll get to later). You can even make the learning process part of your content. Think of all those cooking blogs that chronicle disastrous culinary experiments. Those are fun, right? And a pediatrician who admits he is considering changing his approach to vaccines based on the newest studies coming from the APA isn't giving his patients' families reason not to trust him, he's showing them that he's on top of the latest research.

There's only one test I can suggest if you want to be absolutely sure that the passion around which you're building a brand is also a monetizable product. Can you think of at least fifty blog topics that you're amped to write about it? That's about the minimum number of posts you'll need to give yourself enough time to get a feel for the situation.

That said, I'm convinced that if something is your true passion you can find five hundred things—five hundred interesting things—to say about it. Most people talk themselves out of success before they even start. Their passion is stickers, but they think, "There's no way I can make a hundred grand talking about stickers." That's why you're going to crush it—because you're the type who's going to say, "Stickers? Hell, yes, stickers!"

tell a story

Great content is also all about telling stories, and that's true even if you're in retail or B2B or consumer services. If you're a real-estate agent and your area is Clark, New Jersey, then you should want to tell me everything about Clark that makes it unique. Tell me the story of the town, not just the home you want to sell. Make me care about the place as much as you do. If you're a doctor, tell me about the interesting cases you saw today. Tell me about the trends you're seeing, or give me advice or your opinion about flu shots. If your passion is sales, talk to me about why you love it, your favorite persuasive technique, your most interesting clients, and your biggest challenges. Tell me your story, and if you're good, I'll come back for more. Then I'll tell my friends, and they'll come, and where my friends and I go, the dollars—in the form of ad revenue, sponsorships, and invitations to broaden your platform—will follow. Communicate with me, because whoever is the best communicator will win.

don't lie to yourself

Do you have any idea how many people introduce themselves to me with, "Hi, I'm going to be the next Oprah"? I'm all about being confident, and I respect anyone who's got big ambition. But let's face it, not everyone is going to be Oprah. Everyone has the ability to achieve great self-awareness, but we all occasionally lie to ourselves. Some of us, however, lie to ourselves more than others.

When you start thinking about your livelihood and your passion and the content you want to create, may I suggest looking in the mirror and having the following conversation with yourself?

"Is technology (or candy or marketing or soccer) my ultimate passion?

"Yes.

"Okay. Am I good enough to be the best blogger about tech (or candy or marketing or soccer) in the world?

"Uh . . ."

If you cannot answer both of those questions—Am I sure my passion is what I think it is, and Can I talk about it better than anyone else?—with an emphatic "Yes!" you are not going to win. You're not even going to come in fifth, or ninth, or twelfth, which can also be perfectly respectable, profitable positions.

But didn't I say that anyone who creates a blog around his passion can monetize? I did. But a lot of people are good at deluding themselves. And if you go into this deluding yourself, you're not going to make the money and you're not going to be happy and you're going to be just another boring blog on the Internet.

You can monetize any passion, but the level at which you can monetize will be affected by the size of your niche and whether you are able to differentiate yourself enough from the other players in it. There are a lot of pockets out there today, however, that can sustain a nice forty-to-seventy-five-thousand-dollar-a-year business.

---

choose your medium carefully

We've all watched and read and listened to boring blogs. Most of them out there, in fact, are really boring. Is it because the star doesn't know what he's talking about? No—he's on message, he's relevant, he's informative. The problem isn't that he doesn't know what he's talking about, it's that he's talking about it at all. He probably should be talking about something else, something that makes him shine, that gets him excited, that allows his personality and his passion to burst through your monitor and demand that you pay attention no matter whether he's an introvert or an extrovert.

A lot of people add these blogs to their websites for visual interest and to offer a different way for their audience to get information, and that's fine. But adding video or audio elements just for the sake of adding them isn't going to send your brand and business to the moon. The only way these tools work is if you're using them for the right job. Even the dullest introvert has pizzazz when talking about something he is passionate about, and when he's using the right medium to talk about it. If you watch an engineer talking about engineering, and it's boring, one of three problems is in play: he's talking about the wrong topic, he's using the wrong medium, or both. If I spent an hour with him, maybe we'd discover that his medium is writing, and his passion is baseball. Get him writing about baseball, and I guarantee he'll get better feedback and financial results than he ever had when talking about engineering.

There are people who belong in front of a camera, there are people who belong in print, and there are people who belong on the air. These are the extraordinary people. The ordinary ones, the ones like the vast majority of businesspeople and entrepreneurs out there, don't have the showman DNA. That doesn't mean they won't succeed, as long as they are realistic about what success is going to look like. The extraordinary people will makes millions of dollars and the ordinary Joes will earn more in the midfive-figure range. Is that disappointing? Think of it this way: Oprah, who is without a doubt extraordinary, built her brand using the right medium and the right topic, and she made billions, and the massive majority made zero. Today, everybody else can make $40,000 to a million, so long as they can nail the correct combination of their medium and passion. In most of the country, earning midfive figures means you're living pretty well, often exactly as well as you would were you schlepping into someone else's office every day. Now though, you're earning the same money talking about something you are crazy about. It's a good deal. Take it.

Know yourself. Choose the right medium, choose the right topic, create awesome content, and you can make a lot of money being happy.

the lure and the lasso

You're going to work your content in two ways. The first is as a lure, creating it, posting it, and allowing people to come to you as they discover it. The second is to use it as a lasso through comments on other people's content that relates to yours, inserting yourself into existing conversations and actively creating reasons for your audience to come to you. Of course, you have to give people a place to find your killer content, so let's go there next.

---

six

choose your platform

S o you've got a killer product or service and content, now you're going to deliver your message via a blog. In the online world, you've got three formats to choose from, though some people might do a combination: video, audio, or written word.

There is a ton of information already out there detailing the minutiae of how to use all of these platforms. Rather than waste your time here repeating what's already been said, I've recommended in this chapter some of the best resources available. I'd much rather make sure you understand the global implications of these platforms. That said, the next three chapters offer general descriptions and explanations of all the building blocks you'll need to build a successful business through social media. In chapter 10 you'll find an in-depth example of personal brand building that incorporates just about every concept and technique we discuss.

This step in building your business is once again all about working with your DNA. To my mind the most effective content medium is video, and that's the one I prefer to focus on. It's just easier to grab people's attention and draw them in, especially a public who reads less and less. I also think letting people see you is a major plus when you're trying to sell a personal brand. Don't think any subject is off-limits for a video blog. If your passion is sales, do a show about sales. Can you imagine Sam the Salesman who picks a new selling opportunity every day? On Monday he sells flowers, on Tuesday he heads to the flea market, and so on throughout the week. Or maybe he takes a new job and chronicles his rise to salesman of the year. If you're an accountant, you can still put out a video. I sure as hell don't want to read accounting materials, but I'd watch a video if you were good enough to make something like balance sheets or operating profit interesting and you infused your show with personality and everything that makes you unique. Do that and your audience will find you. I guarantee it.

I use video because I love to talk and I've got a big personality and that medium is the most fun for me. But again, do not compromise your DNA. If you're self-conscious in front of a camera but have loads of personality plus a compelling voice, don't force yourself to do a video blog, do an audio podcast. Think about it; it's not just car buffs who listen to *Car Talk*'s Click and Clack, who have a weekly radio show but also a podcast on NPR. They're so funny, charismatic, and knowledgeable they could talk in those

Boston accents about nothing but carburetors all day long and keep people's attention. Do the same thing for photography, or coffee, or soap, or scuba diving. If you have a squeaky voice or you're shy but a brilliant writer, obviously a written blog is the perfect medium for you. By now there are plenty of success stories about people who monetized their awesome blogs. Why can't that be you?

There are other advantages to blogs. They increase the ability for people to find you through Internet searches because their content changes and expands daily. Not so with a website. Publishing a webpage can be very labor intensive and even require learning new software, but a parrot can put up a blog page. It's easy, it's customizable, and it's free. What more do you want?

Even if you already have an ecommerce website or your focus is B2B, you need to start a blog (though once you see how simple it is to do, you may ditch your website altogether). Think of it this way: your website is for communicating logistics and facilitating sales; your blog is for communicating the essence of your brand. It allows you to expand on your topic in ways that a static website simply can't. For example, if you are a software company, your website will explain what products and services you provide, but on your audio podcast you can discuss your thoughts on current software trends, or you can interview company leaders who use your products, and even some who don't, to explore the topic more fully. Giving people interested in software the opportunity to get to know you as a living, thinking, interesting human being who happens to know everything they want to know about software will make them that much more likely to want to do business with you.

Your blog will be your main home, your central location with a no-exceptions open-door policy where anyone can find you. It also serves as storage for all the content you will create, essentially building an archive where people can see how you and your business have evolved and expanded. It is the place where you can talk as loud and as long and as often and as in-depth as you want.

To keep people coming to this home, you need to be constantly reaching out and interacting with the online community of people interested in your passion who are also your potential constituents. To do that, you'll need to step up to one of the many online platforms where you will do the bulk of your marketing and social networking.

the must-haves

In December 2008, I spent $7,500 to offer free shipping codes for Winelibrary.com via three marketing/advertising channels—a perfectly placed billboard on the New Jersey Turnpike, direct mail, and radio. The billboard brought in a hundred and seventy orders. The radio campaign did about two hundred and forty orders. Through direct mail we got a little over three hundred. I Twittered out—for free—a free shipping code and got seventeen hundred orders in forty-eight hours. What this anecdote should prove to you is that platforms are everything, and that the old ones are softening. If they don't adjust soon, they will be gone or at best irrelevant. As it is, these traditional platforms should be only used by the biggest of companies who can afford the scale.

Television, newspapers, and radio used to be the global platforms. Through these channels, companies and a few lucky, connected individuals could distribute their content to the world within a few days. Now, though, all of those platforms have been overshadowed by the biggest global platform ever, the Internet. Within this global platform are social marketing subplatforms, and these are the tools you're going to use to distribute your killer content and your personal brand to the masses, not in days, but in seconds.

The difference between promoting your brand via traditional marketing and advertising mediums and doing it via social networking platforms is like the difference between sending a message by Pony Express and chatting on Instant Messenger. Sure, you could use the former, but there's a good chance the recipient will have moved on and forgotten about you by the time the message arrives at its destination.

We're bordering on social network platform overload. There are fifty or sixty platforms that people are currently using to distribute business content, and by the time this book comes out there will be more, but there are only a few major players with which you need to familiarize yourself. Some have funny names, but otherwise they are no different from the hammers and buckets of paint and fax machines and telephones that people have used for generations to build businesses and spread the word about what they have to offer. The rest of this chapter offers an overview of the leading social marketing platforms and the optimal way to use them.

wordpress and tumblr

All other platforms lead to this one—your home, your destination, your blog. Wordpress and Tumblr are the best and most popular blogging platforms currently available. There are others of course—Blogger and especially Six Apart products are good (and there is smoke at Six Apart, so by the time this book comes out they may be in the game)—but these are two that I have used and liked. Wordpress is the established leader with the most users. Its design is a little busy, it requires a few more steps to get your content up and shared, but it's not difficult to learn. With some practice, in fact, there are some really interesting options available to skilled users, although to my mind there's no reason to bother becoming that skilled. One of its nicest features is an excellent and easy archive system with a search capability, so people can find anything you've ever posted. And Wordpress allows for some sophisticated customization to your page. I'm a big fan of the "themes," too. These are the design options you get to choose from when you create your page, and I think they're really elegant.

Tumblr, on the other hand, is a very simply designed site that is supereasy to use. You can post video and photos on Wordpress, but Tumblr directs you to a template designed specifically for the kind of content you wish to create, whether text, photo, link, video, or music. Hit "Create Post" and you're good to go.

It's a little known fact, too, that Tumblr is the only blogging platform that will host your domain name for free, which can save you hundreds of dollars a year. What this means is that you can identify yourself as Sallydressdesigner.com (you have to buy your name from GoDaddy.com first) instead of Sallydressdesigner.tumblr.com. You have that option on Wordpress, too—sallydressdesigner.com or Sallydressdesigner.wordpress.com—but if you forgo the company name, you have to pay hosting fees.

Another advantage to Tumblr is the reblog function. On Wordpress you have to write a new post about a story you read in order to tell others about it. When account users see somebody post something that they like on Tumblr, they can hit a button above the story that says "reblog," which allows them to "tumble" it. With that, they're using your blog to extend someone else's story. That is exactly the kind of 2.0 word of mouth you want to inspire in your audience so they will do the same for you.

E-mail me at Gary@vaynermedia.com for details about the press conference I'm going to have to explain why I'm a fan of Tumblr.

When using this platform, the most important thing to consider is the user interface of your blog. Consider the "following" buttons as the displays to your storefront—they are what will turn one visit into repeat business.

call-to-action buttons

These incredibly important buttons are all about capture. "Subscribe to Email," "Friend Me Up," "Follow Me," "Become a Fan"—all of these are ways to suggest that your users prolong their interaction with your brand. When you're working your butt off on your social networks to bring your community into your domain, it's so that they will click on one or several of these buttons. If you tried getting people to friend you or follow you via Facebook or Twitter, you'd come across as spam. In the top right corner of my blog I now have a button that says, "Buy my book." Can you imagine how obnoxious I'd look if I sent out tweets every day urging that call to action? Instead, I use the other tools in my toolbox to bring viewers back to my blog, where I knock their socks off with my content, which inspires them to hit the "Buy My Book" call-to-action button and convert a blog visit into a chance to further build my brand and my revenue.

share functions

These are about word of mouth. They are the buttons on your site that make it easy for your viewers to share your content with their social networks—"Stumble Upon," "Digg," "Reddit," "Facebook," "Email This." You use them to lead your users to the well, empowering them to quickly and easily distribute your content for you if they find it exciting and interesting.

If you feel uncertain about how to use any of the platforms discussed in this book—or anything at all, really—all you have to do is google your question. Someone out there has likely had the same problem or query you do and the answer is almost certainly out there for you to find. YouTube is often an even better resource because it often provides "how-to" content in visual form. You can also use Twitter to great effect. I'm not directing you to Google and YouTube and Twitter because I'm lazy, by the way. I'm doing it because I want you to see for yourself how all the information you'll ever need is right at your fingertips. I know you were hoping for some links and resources, but if I'm going to teach you how to fish properly, I can't bait the hook for you. That said, you know where you can reach me directly: gary@vaynermedia.com.

facebook

You've surely heard of Facebook. In the past five years it's become the fastest-growing social networking site in the world, attracting everyone from preteens keeping tabs on the next party to grandmas reuniting with their Girl Scout troops. From Facebook you can share photographs, articles, videos, as well as information about where you've traveled and what music you're listening to, however much of your private life you want people to know. It's an easy, fun platform, yet it also provides you with two places from which you can talk about your business: (1) your normal profile, which might also tell people that you are a member of the group Kitesurfing for Entrepreneurs, that you took a personality quiz revealing that the movie character you most resemble is Chewbacca, and that you are looking forward to hearing Bruce in concert tomorrow night, and (2) a fan page.

If you are in commerce, if you are reading this book, you have to have a Facebook fan page. Why, when your user profile can offer the exact same information? Because your profile only has a five-thousand-person friend limit. So if you're like me and trying to build brand equity, you don't want to have to turn down your nineteen thousand pending friend requests, which would be bad business and also make you look like a jerk. Whoever heard of a business with a five-thousand-customer limit? Your fan page also allows you to e-mail everyone in one shot and allows people to interact with your page. If they join your page or post anything on it, it shows up on the newsfeed—"Gary Vaynerchuk is a fan of Carpenter Bob"—and my friends see, which can lead to curiosity, which can lead to a visit to Carpenter Bob's page, where they see business-related status updates, photos of his craftsmanship, and a link to his blog where they can watch video of him working while he tells how he came up with his newest design for a three-legged dining room table, which leads to an opportunity to make a sale. Eventually the director of the American Society of Furniture Designers might visit Carpenter Bob's blog and invite him to speak at the group's next conference. Then *Dwell* magazine calls. Next thing Bob knows, he's earning money building his beautiful tables as well as profiting by talking about his tables all around the country. Thanks, Facebook.

If you've been using a regular profile or created a group for your business, don't take it down. Simply leave a link on your old profile or group page that feeds to your new fan page.

Though your fan page should always stay on a business-oriented message, some people use their personal profile pages to talk about their business, too. That's entirely up to you and your DNA. What you do with Facebook (and Twitter, which we'll talk about next) should be an absolute reflection of how you live in your daily life. Experienced businesspeople already know that most networking and brand building is done in casual environments— at the ball game, at a picnic, while untangling the dogs when they cross leashes. If you talk shop at every cocktail party, strike up conversations with seatmates on airplanes, or hand your card out at your cousin's wedding, then your personal profile should also update everyone who comes to you about what's going on with your business. It's just an extension of everyday life. You should occasionally mix things up, though, and let people in so they get a feel for your personality. It's totally possible to include a healthy mix of updates, like "I love scrapple for breakfast," with "Just sold my millionth unit," or "In two hours I'm hosting an online semi-nar on interactive media. Who's in?" The most important thing to remember is to be authentic, to be yourself. That authenticity is what will give you your greatest chance of success.

There are privacy settings on Facebook that allow you to compartmentalize groups of contacts and friends so that some can only see certain parts of your Facebook page, like the in-formation page where you might put your professional history, and not others, like your status updates where you might men-tion you're hungover. I'd love for you to ignore privacy settings because I don't think it's useful to place restrictions on your brand, but if it makes you uncomfortable to expose yourself to the world that much, go ahead and use the filter. There is an inherent business cost, but business costs should never trump personal costs.

twitter

By the time you read this, Twitter will have become a main verb—people will tweet just like everyone googles and xeroxes. Like Facebook, you use Twitter to put out content, albeit bite-sized—140 characters, max—and to follow other people's bite-sized content.

Some people react to Twitter with disbelief. "Who the heck wants to know that I'm on my way to get a pedicure, or that I'm thinking fish sticks for dinner?" But the day I saw it I knew I was staring at the pulse of society; it was the most game-changing website I'd ever seen prior to Facebook. You think people are confused by it now? You should have seen people scratching their heads over it in 2007 when I first started using and talking about it. Here's what I know: many people do want to know all the details about what you're doing and thinking, they just don't want to admit it. We've all got our voyeuristic tendencies; Twitter has just given us permission to cave in to them. But the fact that you can share your dinner preferences with thousands of people instantaneously is not even in the top five reasons Twitter is perhaps the most powerful brand-building tool in your toolbox.

First, it has incredible endorsement power. When someone re-tweets what you say, they're saying you're smart and worth paying attention to. That comes with a lot of value. The re-tweet enables anyone to spread whatever content they find profound or solid or funny or good throughout the world in a very quick and efficient way. Tumblr has the tumble option, which is similar, but Twitter is sizzling hot and mainstream and there are way more eyeballs on it. From the beginning it was developed to be a mobile platform, so even though Facebook has an app you can use from your phone, Twitter has so much brand equity already in place as the on-the-go social network that most people use it first.

Second, it's a press release opportunity, allowing companies and businesses to have a closer relationship with their consumer. It closes the six degrees of separation to one degree of separation. It's also become a basic tool for industry leaders to let the world know what they're doing and, perhaps more important, what's on their mind. And it allows companies to respond immediately to their customers' concerns. For example, as soon as I read somebody's post that my shipping rates were too expensive, I was immediately able to reach out and address that person's concern. We'll be seeing more and more examples of companies reacting to a groundswell of tweets, such as when Motrin got hammered by mom-bloggers for an ad that they perceived as disrespectful of attachment parenting, or when Amazon fended off accusations of censorship via what the *New York Times* dubbed "tweet-rage" because a "cataloging error" erased thousands of books, many of them gay and lesbian themed, from its sales rankings and main search page. The thing is, though, businesses don't have to, nor should they, wait until calamity strikes to pay attention to what people are saying. The real beauty of Twitter and Facebook (and all the other social networking sites) is that they offer a massive opportunity for every entrepreneur and business to keep constant tabs on what their customers are thinking about them. This kind of interaction with the consumer should be happening in every business every single day.

Third, Twitter is a research and development tool that allows you to crowdsource. Who needs focus groups or even Nielsen ratings when you can simply tweet out the question "Are you watching *Poodles Dancing with the Stars* and should it stay on the air?" and get a direct response from your viewers? You can use Twitter to keep abreast of what your competition is up to, and their customers' reactions, too. Saks recently opened a shoe department in New York and worked with the post office to assign it its own zip code. If I were working at Bloomingdale's or Bergdorf, I would have been all over Search.Twitter (see upcoming information) to see what people were saying about this marketing program.

Fourth, it allows even your most mundane questions to become opportunities for conversation. Google and YouTube are reliable ways to get information, but they're one-way streets. You ask, you get your answer, the end. You can send out e-mails, but then you're limited to the immediate group of people you know. But if you tweet "Is there a PowerPoint expert out there?," you're reaching out to thousands of people, and the first thing they'll want to know when they respond is what you're presenting, and to whom, which opens up all kinds of chances to talk about what you do and who you are and bingo, you're building brand equity. Twitter is a two-way street that takes you really far, really fast.

Fifth, it's a great vehicle through which to spread your commerce-driven intentions. If you're reading this book, you've got commerce-driven intentions—you want to build a brand, sell a product, find a job. Get those intentions on Twitter, and you'll be amazed at how people respond.

The best use for Twitter, though, is to lure people to your blog. Make your 140-character tweets compelling and thoughtful and quality enough to convince people to find out more about you and consume your content. You can post great content on Twitter—several people have used Twitter to incredible effect to build their brand equity—but because of the 140-character limit you have to tweet out a lot in order to have the same amount of impact with your content as you would with your blog. Plus, there's always the risk of being perceived as spam when you tweet that much. I think it's more efficient and effective to link tweets to your blog. Even those individuals known for their presence on Twitter have links to blogs. Chris Sacca is a master tweeter, but he does keep a blog. Granted, he only blogs about once a month. He hasn't asked for my opinion, but I think he could build even more brand equity if he blogged every day. That would give people even more reasons to hang with him. To each his own DNA, however.

If you're not using Twitter because you're in the camp that believes it's stupid, you're going to lose out. It doesn't matter if you think it's stupid, it's free communication. That in and of itself has value, and you should take advantage of it. Use Twitter the same way you use your cell phone or a map or a GPS—it's one more tool to get you closer to the people and places you need.

For inspiration go to Chris Brogan's "50 Ideas on Using Twitter for Business": http://www.chrisbrogan.com/50-ideas-on-using-twitter-for-business/

For a very low cost of entry and time Twitter allows the consumer to tell every person in his world what he thinks is cool or crappy or interesting. Do your job right, and eventually you can be the cool, interesting subject that gets circulated, which will bring viewers to your blog, which will get the attention of people with deep pockets. Ten years ago it would have taken you months if not years to generate that kind of word of mouth. Today it takes seconds.

I want to share with you the best business tweet of all time:

"What can I do for you?"

You'll be amazed at the response you get. You're in business to serve your community. Don't ever forget it.

As of May 2009, when this book went to press, Search.Twitter.com is the most important site on the Internet. Search.Twitter gives you the ability to narrow in on the pulse of subject matter. For example, let's say you work for Wyeth Consumer Healthcare, specifically for Advil. Go to Search.Twitter.com and enter the word *headache*, or enter the word in the search box on the right side of your Twitter page. You can now see that twenty people in the last three minutes have used the word *headache* in their tweet, including a woman named Jillian who writes, "Terrible headache. Someone hand me a sledgehammer." You can click on the button that says "Follow." If they choose to follow you back, you can now privately direct message (DM) her or publicly send her an @reply, with a message that might read like this: "Hey Jillian, I work for Advil and saw that you have a headache. Sorry to hear it. I'd love to send you a bottle of our product. DM me back with your address if you're interested." Most people will jump on the chance to get free product, and you have just created the most intimate experience with a brand anyone has ever known. If I do a search right now, I find that fifteen people in the last twenty-three minutes have said they're thirsty. This is a golden opportunity for someone in the sports drink business, or the bottled water business, or the wine business.

But how do you avoid annoying people, or worse, sounding like spam? Everybody has a different idea of what's annoying—I don't mind hearing from someone interested in sending me free stuff that I can actually use. And remember that the only way you, the content provider, can contact anyone is if they choose to follow you—you cannot DM them otherwise. It's the equivalent of extending your hand and allowing someone to choose whether to shake (you can certainly use @reply, but to me that's like yelling, "Hey, you!" instead of offering a handshake; it's just a little less polite). You also want to pitch your message in a very proactive, cool way. You're not telling Jillian to go buy the stuff; you're giving her a chance to try it if she wants it. You're also not hiding your affiliation with your company and brand. If someone chooses to follow you, they'll see on your profile that you're a manager on the Advil brand. If you stay aboveboard and honest, most people will be willing to listen to what you have to say about your product. But the second you DM someone and they decide you sound slimy, they'll un-follow you. Their bs detector is better than any spam filter you've ever seen. Don't betray their trust.

If your blog is your home, platforms like Twitter and Facebook are your vacation homes. You can't do long form content on these sites (well, you can, but it's not effective and I don't recommend it), and you need someplace that is a free place to do business where people don't have to be members to see you. Your content permanently resides on your blog, and you use these platforms to distribute your brand and bring eyes back home.

When this book became available for presale, I used both Twitter and Facebook to bring eyes back to my blog and, crucially, to convert my call-to-action buttons into brand-building opportunities. Here's how: I posted a video on my blog excitedly making the announcement. I talked about what the book is about and why it means so much to me. Along with the expected links to B&N and Amazon, I included a line that said "Pass This Book on to Your Friends," with links to Twitter and Facebook below. If you chose Twitter, you found a prewritten tweet to send out that included a link back to my blog and in particular the video announcing the book. If you chose Facebook, you came upon a message box where you could write a post, then update your page with the link to my blog attached. In addition, I included a button on my blog that said "Support Gary's Book," which led you to a new page in which I thanked you for your interest and provided a widget of the book that you could add to your own website or blog. That page also included the links to Twitter and Facebook, and, as always, my e-mail address.

Though as you can tell I'm a huge fan of Twitter and Facebook, they are becoming household names and the competition there is already fierce, so I'm considering a new strategy. Why not explore some other Facebook-like sites even though they have fewer fish in their pond? True, the ponds are smaller, but their banks aren't swarming with other fishermen, either, which means you have a much better chance at walking away with a hefty catch. Some sites that I'm watching closely are the following:

- Plaxo, a professional site
- High Five
- Bebo, which is big in the UK and the third-biggest social network behind Facebook and MySpace
- FriendFeed
- Orkut, which is huge in Brazil

flickr

This photo-sharing site is definitely a pond worth fishing in. It has a ton of passionate users, though I'm not one of them for the sole reason that photographs don't speak to my DNA. They do a lot for plenty of other people, though. Any platform that has loads of search capabilities is an important place to find market opportunity, and there are millions of people searching on Flickr. As with all content, you work the content on this site in two ways. You can post photographs so that when people click on them they find out who you are and then follow your link back to your blog, or you can click on other people's photos and leave comments that intrigue people enough to link back to you. If your passion is something that photographs well, like birds or jewelry or hairstyling or interior design, it's a place where you can do a lot of good damage. If I throw a wine party, I can post pictures of the event, which could pique someone's interest. Or, if I put up a label of every wine I discuss on my show, I could conceivably draw a lot more traffic to my blog. In fact, now that I think about it, it's insane that I haven't done this already. Anyone who cares about wine should be able to find me on Flickr, so I'd better get on that.

I admire Moo (www.moo.com) because they have used Flickr and Facebook to reinvent old, tired products—business cards, notecards, and stickers. Customers can use their own photos or upload images from any of Moo's partner sites. You can even print a different image on every card within a single pack, allowing you to let people choose their favorite one and creating a ready-made conversation piece around your brand. It goes to show that any product can be huge when approached from a new angle.

youtube and/or viddler

These are both video platforms that I use and like. YouTube is like the ocean—it's huge, you go out in it, and you can come home with a boatload of fish. But you're also competing against millions of fishermen. Viddler is much smaller, which allows you to see and be seen with greater ease. It also allows you to brand your player, so that anyone who watches the video sees only your logo at the bottom, which I think has value. If you use YouTube, the YouTube logo appears at the bottom of all of their videos. Viddler also allows you to tag your video, which means you can earmark important moments for your viewers by placing a little dot within the video stream linked to a key word, allowing for easier searches should someone want to see a particular part of the video without sitting through the whole thing. For example, if I do a thirty-minute wine show and am discussing three wines, and you're only interested in the third wine, you can go straight to that segment of the video because I'll have marked within the video stream where my review of each wine begins.

YouTube has a larger user base, which can definitely be an advantage. You can embed from either site, which is as easy to do as copying and pasting the embed code. I do give Viddler an enthusiastic thumbs-up for the way it takes care of its users. Have you ever wondered how certain videos get featured on these sites' homepages? YouTube is so huge and so swamped with video submissions that featured videos are usually a result of random luck, biz dev, and inside deals. Because Viddler is smaller, however, their staff is quickly able to assess new talent on their network and support that talent by featuring it on their homepage. Viddler doesn't wait for you to make it big; they'll give you a shot for a day or two if they think you're good enough. They're great at identifying talent early on.

ustream.tv

There is no way to overstate the importance of Ustream, one of the biggest brand-building products that I've used. It's a platform that allows you to launch live video, but the cool part is that it also has a chat function that allows you to interact with your audience in real time, much like a radio call-in show.

How does the content you post on Ustream differ from what you post on your video blog, if that's your preferred medium?

Think of your blog as a formal presentation, a prepared speech about a predetermined topic in which you control the message and all the content. Once you've said your piece, you're done. If anyone wishes to challenge you or ask for clarification or comment, they certainly can, but some time will pass before they get their answer. By the time you get back to them, you may have to remind them what they asked you in the first place. And if you decide to address their questions in a follow-up video, you have to hope that they come back to hear what you have to say.

Your Ustream video allows you to talk about your brand the way you might at a cocktail party during which you get a chance to work the room and find out what's on everybody's mind. By responding to chats while you livestream you can establish the most powerful—and empowering—interactive brand experience any consumer has ever known. Even live television can't provide this kind of immediacy. It's so sticky—people love to know they can come talk to you one-on-one. Best of all, it costs you nothing. Ustream is another classic example of an Internet platform that costs the brand and product nothing to use yet provides amazing return on investment.

Natasha Wescoat is an artist known for her candied landscapes and whimsical characters. She is rising in popularity as a result of using social media tools to connect with her audience and engage with her collectors and potential buyers. As a result, her business has grown 50 percent in six months and her business network 80 percent. In addition to Twitter, she uses Ustream.tv to livestream her painting in the studio. It began as an experiment but within a week she had viewers buying directly from her LIVE online. Since then, she has used it as a tool for studio sales and auctions. By allowing her viewers to watch her create something, it inspires them to buy directly, then and there.

word-of-mouth power moves

There are a few additional tools that can add a real boost to your word-of-mouth potential.

Just as it would be a shame to decide that Chardonnay is your favorite wine when you've hardly tried any other varietal, you should try every platform to see which ones work best for you. Now, when I was just getting started, Chris Mott, my camera guy, had to spend hours every night individually uploading the blog onto every single platform we were using. Luckily, there are now two sites that are going to make life a lot easier for you.

Ping.fm is a service that allows you to post a limited amount of text, such as a status update, one time, and then automatically distributes the update to any of over thirty social networking sites, including Twitter, Facebook, Tumblr, Flickr, Wordpress, Jaiku, Friendfeed, MySpace, and Del.icio.us. Currently the service doesn't allow for video, but according to the site that capability is coming soon.

If you are a video blogger, you must have a TubeMogul account. It's a website that allows you to upload your video once, then distributes it to countless video-sharing sites for free. It's also a tracking service, offering analytics about who is watching your videos, when, from what sites, and how often.

Analytics

I use analytics very rarely and I urge you not to rely too much on them either, especially if you've got good business instincts. A lot of times the stats and percentages related to my business just don't support what my instinct says is true, and I'll trust my instincts over numbers every time. What if your analytics tell you that you've only had seven views on Break.com in two months? Are you going to stop posting to that platform? The data are telling you that you should probably drop it, but what you don't know is that one of those seven viewers is a producer for *The Today Show*. There's no reason to think that can't happen.

The numbers can be a trap that changes your behavior. People see they've only gotten fifty viewers in a few weeks and decide they suck and they stop trying as hard. Or their video catches on and gets watched a thousand times and they think they've made it, and they stop trying as hard. Metrics can be useful, of course, but the effect of your online interactions and the excitement building toward your brand isn't accurately reflected by the number of viewers you have. It's not about how many viewers you have, it's about how passionate they are. If you must use them, analytics should remain a minor-league detail. Focus the majority of your attention on your overall brand positioning.

Facebook Connect is a service that allows new users of your site to skip the long process of registering personal information—how many hundreds of times have you filled in boxes asking for your name, address, password, and so on, by now?—by pulling it from their Facebook page. It will also pull Facebook profile data to save them the slog of having to fill out yet again all of the personal and professional information onto the new site. So Facebook Connect is a huge time-saver for your viewers. In addition, when a Facebook member clicks "Connect with Facebook," an announcement will be sent to her friends' Facebook newsfeed and on her wall that she is now a user of your site. By now you should know why that's a good thing—people with similar tastes to your new user see that newsfeed and think, "Hm, what's that?" and then come see you for themselves. If you're telling your story well and putting out awesome content, there's no reason they won't return and bring more friends with them.

We're going to see a lot more of Facebook Connect in the future. It allows such quick interaction and site building that it has the potential to become as omnipresent and necessary as your cell phone and e-mail account.

For a comprehensive list of many more tools and applications, go to www.somewhatfrank.com/2008/12/social-media-my.html

And check out these blogs:

TechCrunch

ReadWriteWeb

GigaOm

SocialTimes

Endgaget

---

differentiate yourself

Everything we've talked about in this book so far—passion, knowing yourself, personal branding, word of mouth—has always been important to every successful business in history. These social networking sites have only changed the game by giving entrepreneurs a reason to ditch the sinking traditional media and advertising platforms in favor of a communication method that opens them up to markets that would have been inaccessible until just a few short years ago.

The thing is, just having a presence on these platforms doesn't get you any further ahead of the competition because most entrepreneurs are getting wise to the need of having a Twitter and Facebook account, not to mention all the other platforms we've discussed. So how are you going to differentiate yourself from all the other clowns? ("Clowns" is, of course, used in the best possible way.) You're going to do your content better, and you're going to do it your way using the tools we just discussed.

Vitamins can give your body a real boost, but they won't do you much good if you don't also incorporate exercise, proper nutrition, and even vaccines into your healthy habits. The same goes for all of these platforms. Each one individually gives your personal brand strength and reach, but if you use them together properly, they can turn you into a force to be reckoned with.

The other thing you're going to do is accept that just having good content and Internet access is not enough to take your business to the top. There are a lot of people who have good content, and everyone has the same access to the same tools as you do. What they don't have (though they think they might), and what we'll talk about in the next chapter, makes all the difference. After all, lots of people can play the piano, but not everyone can be Billy Joel.

---

seven

keep it real . . . very real

authenticity

We've talked about paying attention to your DNA, but while the concept of authenticity is closely related it's not the same. Your DNA dictates your passion—whatever it is you were born to do; being authentic, and being perceived as such by your audience, relies on your ability to ensure that every decision you make when it comes to your business is rooted in being true to yourself.

For example, I would love to change the opening of my show. It starts off the same almost every time. "HELLO EVERYBODY AND WELCOME TO WINE LIBRARY TV. I AM YOUR HOST GARY VAY-NER-CHUK AND THIS, MY FRIENDS, IS THE THUNDER SHOW AKA THE INTERNET'S MOST PASSIONATE WINE PROGRAM." It's not exactly what some wine lovers are looking for in a wine expert, and I lose about 12 percent of my viewers right off the bat because I yell and scream like a maniac. For a businessman like me, that number is intolerable. I desperately want to change the opening of my show to something a little calmer, more refined, something that won't scare people away. But I can't, because that yelling, screaming, superexcited guy is who I am. If I tried to tone things down and make myself appealing to that missing 12 percent, I can guarantee that everything I've built until now would start slipping away, because now every time I'd get in front of that Flip Cam I'd be putting on an act. I'm not putting on a performance when I do the show or my blog posts—I'm just being me.

invest in the important stuff

One of the silliest questions I get is, "What kind of mic do you use?" To that I reply, why are you even worrying about that? Your content has nothing to do with the mic, the camera, the lighting, or the set. The day I filmed my first Thunder Show I sent the stock boy out to buy a $400 video camera from Best Buy (now I use a fancy Sony that cost a few thousand bucks, but most of my recent shows I tape on a $150 Flip Cam and they look fine). Watch the show, what do you see? It's me, sometimes an awesome guest ranging from my dad to Wayne Gretzky to Jim Cramer, some bottles of wine, and a Jets spit bucket. I only invest effort and thought into what I care about and what I need to create great content.

My business blog, Garyvaynerchuk.com, is even less dressed up. A lot of times I'm filming from my office, which is usually a mess. I could clean it up to look more professional and polished, but it seems wrong to do that just because the Flip Cam is running. There's nothing scripted and nothing staged about my blogs, and I always, always do only one take. No redos, no tweaks, nothing. People walk in and out of the office, I wave to folks passing in the hall—whatever happens during filming is what my audience will see. I've filmed posts from balconies, hotel rooms, the street, even my editor's office—anywhere an idea strikes me. Sometimes the sound quality sucks. Sometimes the light is bad. As long as I get my point across and feel like I delivered the message in an authentic way, I don't care.

Once upon a time the most popular celebrities were boxed up in such slick, sleek packages it was almost impossible to get a feel for their real personalities. Every move was choreographed, even their love lives, and even when they weren't on the red carpet they were red-carpet ready. Those days are long gone. The celebrities of today, the ones who are making it huge by connecting with their fans, whether on the screen or online, are all about keeping it real and being themselves. No matter how big or small you want to go, your authenticity will be at the root of your appeal and is what will keep people coming to your site and spreading the word about your personal brand, service, or whatever you are offering.

If you want to dominate the social media game, all of your effort has to come from the heart; and it can't come from the heart in the passionate, irrational, wholehearted way it needs to if you're trying to be anyone but yourself. Authenticity is what will make it possible for you to put in the kind of hustle necessary to crush it.

hustle

I've said over and over that if you live your passion and work the social networking tools to the max, opportunities to monetize will present themselves. I've also said that in order to crush it you have to be sure your content is the best in its category. You can still make plenty of good money if you're fourth best in a category, or ninth best, but if you really want to dominate the competition and make big bucks, you've got to be the best. Do that, be that, and no one will be able to touch you.

With one exception. Someone with less passion and talent and poorer content can totally beat you if they're willing to work longer and harder than you are. Hustle is it. Without it, you should just pack up your toys and go home.

Now, I'm betting that most people who pick up this book consider themselves hard workers. Many are probably just sick of the killer hours and inflexible schedules and demanding bosses often found in the corporate world and think entrepreneurship will somehow be less taxing. I hate to disappoint, but if you're looking for an easier time here, you're barking up the wrong tree. There might be a little more flexibility to your day should you be at liberty to devote yourself full-time to building your personal brand, but otherwise, assuming you're doing this right, you'll be bleeding out of your eyeballs at your computer. You might have thought your old boss was bad, but if you want your business to go anywhere, your new boss had better be a slave driver.

Too many people don't want to swallow the pill of working every day, every chance they get. If you're making money through social media, you don't get to work for three hours and then play Nintendo for the rest of the evening. That's lip service to hard work. No one makes a million dollars with minimal effort unless they win the lottery.

The cool thing about hustle, though, is that it's one more thing that equalizes the playing field. Fifteen years ago you could have had a rock-solid idea of your DNA and your passion, but there was a billion to one chance of you actually crushing it in business—the platforms and channels were just too narrow and guarded by some pretty tight gatekeepers. Now we can take advantage of the explosion of tremendous, free digital platforms on the Internet, which are also making the gatekeepers more and more irrelevant. And now it's no longer a special interest story if you make it big without family connections or money or an education, because everyone can do it. The only differentiator in the game is your passion and your hustle. Don't ever look at someone else who has more capital or cred than you and think you shouldn't bother to compete. You may only have a million-dollar business, and your biggest competitor may have a fifty-million-dollar business, but if you can outwork him or her, you will win over time.

Anything insane has a price. If you're serious about building your personal brand, there will be no time for Wii. There will be no time for Scrabble or book club or poker or hockey. There will be time for meals, and catching up with your significant other, and playing with the kids, and otherwise you will be in front of your computer until 3:00 A.M. every night. If you're unemployed or retired and have all day to work, maybe you knock off at midnight instead. Expect this to be all consuming.

The thing is, if you're living your passion, you're going to want to be consumed by your work. There's no room for relaxation in the flop-on-the-couch-with-popcorn-and-watch-TV kind of way, but you won't need it. You're not going to be stressed or tired. You're going to be relaxed and invigorated. The passion and love for what you do will enable you to work the hours necessary to succeed. You'll lose track of the time, go to bed reluctantly, and wake up in the morning excited to do it all over again. You'll be living and breathing your content, learning everything you can about your subject, about your tools, about your competition, and talking nonstop with other people interested in the same thing you are.

As hard as you're going to push yourself, don't plan on seeing results right away.

I'd say that this leads us to the number one issue that trips up a lot of otherwise savvy entrepreneurs trying to build their brand online.

patience

Ninety percent of the people I hear from are in complaint mode, usually to the tune of, "I'm working hard and I'm crushing it and nothing's happening. What gives?" So I ask, how long have you been at this? And they'll usually answer something like, "Six weeks." Six weeks? You don't build businesses in six weeks, or two months, or six months. If you contact me within a year of starting your business to complain that you haven't made the money you thought you would, you're not listening. I said that you could make a ton of money being happy; I didn't say you could do it overnight.

People listen to me talk about what it takes to monetize their personal brand and sometimes I think they filter out the parts they don't want to hear. They think, *I've got the passion, I can do hustle like nobody else. Patience? Leave that for the other guys— I'm gonna turbocharge this sucker.* But patience is the secret sauce. Once you put up your site, you don't want to start and stop, backtrack and second-guess. It'll make you look insecure and foolish. If you're patient, you'll be more likely to plan and prepare and make sure everything is in place before making the big moves that are going to monetize your brand to the fullest.

Everyone makes a big deal over the fact that it only took me eighteen months from the time I launched Winelibrarytv.com to getting booked on Late Nite with Conan O'Brien. I started taping episodes in 2006, back before most people were watching online videos. I'm sure if I started the blog today, now that more people have iPhones and are watching online videos, it would take me even less time to get on everyone's radar. Yet as fast as the results seem to have happened, I can assure you that the whole process took a hell of a long time.

You'll recall that I was only sixteen when I started working the floor at Shopper's Discount Liquors selling wine to customers, which meant that I still couldn't drink the stuff. I knew, though, that appreciating wine, and therefore being able to sell it and discuss it confidently, meant developing a great palate. I read all the tasting notes in *Wine Spectator* and started to learn to identify flavor profiles of things that I could easily find at ShopRite, like pear, papaya, cherries, chocolate, and blackberries. I didn't stop there, though. I sought out more exotic fare, like cassis and black raspberry preserve and star fruit (recently I discovered goji berries . . . good stuff). But there was more. Critics noted hints of cigar, and dirt, and even sweaty sock in wine. I knew they were guessing—there was no way they'd sucked on a sweaty sock—and I thought, *Well, if I'm going to say something tastes like sweaty socks, shouldn't I know what it tastes like?* So I gave myself an education. By the time I was twenty-one, I had an incredibly developed palate, even though I hadn't drunk much wine at all.

When I started developing the idea for building Wine Library TV, and later Garyvaynerchuk.com, I knew that I would have to use the same kind of patience and methodology to learn the social media business as I did to learn the wine business.

It was patience that helped me grow Wine Library, too. I was twenty-two years old and running a ten-million-dollar business. I did it with good old-fashioned hustle—every customer who walked in got monetized to the fullest. If they walked in for one bottle, they usually walked out with three. And I was being paid $27,000 a year. Most young people who take a business from four to ten million feel they deserve a watch and a car and a cool apartment as rewards for their savviness and hard work. Get over that. You come last. Before you invest in yourself, you have to invest in your long-term future. That means your profits should funnel right back into your research, your content, and your staff should you have any. The sooner you start cashing in, the shorter window you have in which to cement your success. So hold off as long as you can.

This is why, as ambitious and thirsty as I was for megasuccess as a business developer, I didn't make a peep anywhere the first year and a half that I was airing the show. I didn't try to make one biz dev deal. I probably could have had some success had I jumped the gun, but by remaining patient and making sure I knew exactly what I was doing, I was able to avoid taking any steps backward once the speaking engagements, consulting opportunities, and advertisers started showing up.

How did someone like me, who is so obviously not a patient guy, cool my heels for so long? Because I was 100 percent happy. I loved what I was doing. I knew down to my core that my business was going to explode, but even if I had fallen flat on my face, I would have had no regrets because I was doing exactly what I wanted to do, the way I wanted to do it.

Now do you get why it's so, so important for you to center your business on your passion? If you enter a niche because you're following the dollars, you won't keep it up. It's too much work, and you will get tired and frustrated and you will eventually fold. You have to think about building your brand in terms of a marathon, not a sprint. It will take longer to see results, but in seven or nine or fifteen years you won't crack, you'll still love what you're doing.

What exactly are you going to be doing that's going to be so time and labor intensive? You'll be studying your topic, researching your platforms, drafting your blog posts, doing whatever it takes to become the foremost expert and personal brand in your field. But most of all, you will be creating a community.

eight

create community: digging your internet trench

A lot of people get wrapped up in designing their blogs and writing or taping their content. But creating your content is the easy part. Of course your product should be as good as it can be, but it should also be the least time-consuming element of your whole endeavor. What you do after you tape a show or write or record is the whole game. Creating community—that's where the bulk of your hustle is going to go and where the bulk of your success will be determined.

Creating community is about starting conversations. When you move into a new house, you meet your neighbors by going out in the evenings and shaking hands with people walking their dogs or taking their runs, complimenting people on their gardens, introducing your kids if you notice a family playing in their yard with children of the same age. If you go to a conference, you meet your fellow attendees by introducing yourself and shaking hands with everyone else who's milling about. You trade anecdotes and information, hand out your business card. Creating community online works exactly the same way. To create an audience for your personal brand, you're going to get out there, shake hands, and join every single online conversation already in play around the world about your topic. Every. Single. One.

Jared Montz is a retired professional soccer player who relies heavily on just about every platform we've discussed in this book to build his brand and America's 1st Online Soccer Academy, JMSoccer10.com. Though he barely understood Facebook and didn't have a Twitter account when he started, he now considers them his biggest asset, using them to build a community of soccer fans and friends, draw traffic to his site, and alert followers whenever he posts a new blog, video, or podcast (that's right, he uses all three). "I go to bed at 3:00 A.M., wake up at 6:00 A.M., and spend hours commenting and talking with people about soccer. Not selling them my stuff, but talking about soccer. They will find out what I do on their own without me spamming them." His equipment? A laptop, his fiancée's six-year-old camera, a POS tripod, and his iPhone. Is he crushing it? In his own words, "I'm having a blast! It's fun to meet people and players no matter what, but businesswise the potential is just scary. It takes a lot of blood, sweat, and tears, but if you love it then it's all worth it."

Every subject, no matter how small, has an Internet trench. You need to find it (googling is a way to start). Every night after taping an episode of my show, I'd spend the next eight or nine hours in the Internet wine trenches, digging up as much information as possible about who was talking about wine and wine-related subjects and products—what they were saying, where they were going, who they were reading, what they were drinking, what they were buying, what they were slamming. And then I'd start reaching out.

At a certain point, your business will start gaining eyeballs and your community focus will change. Whereas at this point you're initiating contact with anyone who might have an interest in your passion, later you will spend these late-night hours responding to the people who have responded to you. Building and sustaining community is a never-ending part of doing business.

I would read hundreds of blog posts and leave comments on many of them. I'd spend time on wine forums and read what other people said and then comment on those comments.

You're going to do exactly the same thing. Here's how:

First, create your blog post and distribute it through Tube-Mogul (video) or Ping.fm (links) so that your content appears on every social networking platform available.

Next, start paying attention to other people's content. You're going to use the tools we discussed in the last chapter, like Twitter Search, to seek out every mention of your topic on the Internet, and you're going to comment on every single blog and forum post and tweet that you can find. Now, you're not going to say something just for the sake of saying something. You're an expert, right? You love your topic and you've been doing your research. So you leave expert, intriguing, thoughtful, provocative, intelligent comments with your name and a link back to your blog.

Last, you're going to capture. If you're as good as you should be when you're talking about your passion, people are going to be intrigued by what you have to say. Even if they don't follow you immediately, if they see you appear on their site often enough, they may get curious enough to follow you back to your blog. That's when you've got them.

Y ou know how to solidify your fan base? Pay attention to them. I've picked up the phone to talk to people when it seemed warranted or appropriate. The chalkboard behind me during many wine blog episodes is for my hard-core fans—whatever appears there is a coded message or inside joke just for them. Little gestures like these that say, hey, I see you here, and I appreciate it, carry a lot of value.

---

capture

You just brought someone who's interested in your topic to your blog devoted to that topic. What you do now is exactly the same as I used to do when someone would walk in looking for a bottle of wine and I'd send them home with two cases—you monetize the heck out of every interaction. In this case, you're not giving people something to drink, you're giving them something to think about, and ultimately, to talk about. If your content is smart and interesting and eye-catching and entertaining—and if you're the best, it should be—most people who come to your blog will be happy to become regular readers, viewers, or listeners. Make it easy for them.

We covered the importance of user interface and call-to-action buttons in chapter 6. Call-to-action buttons include:

- Subscribe—allows people to opt in to getting an e-mail every time you post a blog
- Follow Me—keeps viewers apprised of your tweets and status updates
- Join My Fan Page—announces to the viewer's newsfeed that they think enough of you to be a fan and helps put your site on other people's radar
- Share—makes it easy for viewers to post your link on Facebook, MySpace, etc.
- Twitter This
- Email This

Your long-term goal is to get sticky and create more and more opportunities to communicate. Your audience joins your fan page. They comment on your blog. They tweet and tumble your posts. And slowly but surely their friends take notice, and start doing the same, and their friends take notice, and suddenly your little community of one explodes into a major metropolis.

the power of one

How do you know when you've built a community? When one person is listening. Wine Library TV had five viewers at first.

D on't get obsessed with how many friends or fans are following you—the stats are only marginally important. What's important is the intensity of your community's engagement and interaction with you. At this point the quality of the conversation is much more revealing than the number of people having it. If your content is making people talk enough so they start to make some noise, I guarantee you're going to see more people show up to your party. As long as you're seeing your audience grow, even modestly, over the first four or five months, you're doing what you're supposed to do.

The day you see that one person is reading or watching or listening to you is a day to celebrate. It's an amazing thing to know someone gives a crap about what's going on in your world, your life, your brain. Don't take people for granted. The word-of-mouth power in one interested person has unbelievable reach. Believe me, one day you'll miss your small, intimate community where you could carry on sustained conversations and get to know people really well. I know I do. (But I still try to get in there daily.)

next steps

Now that you have a community you've got someplace to put a killer marketing strategy into play. The one I use is the best in the world and has never failed me.

nine

---

the best marketing
strategy ever

CARE.

Got any questions? E-mail me at gary@vaynermedia.com.

ten

make the world listen

Any topic can be turned into a profitable, sustainable social-media-driven business. Let's see how we could pull together all the tools and concepts we've discussed so far to build a business around something really fun and exciting. How about . . .

Accounting.

Let's say you start on a Monday. So on Monday, the first day of the rest of your life, you do the following:

1. Go to GoDaddy.com. and try to buy your name, as in first-namelastname.com. If it's not available, try yourname.tv. Now, I got lucky with a name like Gary Vaynerchuk. Are you a CPA named Robert Smith? Sorry, Robert Smith, you're screwed. Obviously someone has already bought Robertsmith.com or robertsmithcpa.com. Now's the time to get creative. How about BobtheBudgetman.tv?

If you can't come up with anything appropriate or all of your top ideas are unavailable, e-mail me at gary@vaynermedia.com and we'll brainstorm together.

Buy both .com and .tv if possible because you never know if you'll need them and there's no obligation to launch both. While you're at it, buy the domain names for your children if you can. In addition, note that every time you hear about a new platform that looks like it's going to go mainstream, you'll have to register your user name (Twitter.com/BobtheBudgetman, Facebook.com/BobtheBudgetman, etc.).

I see no reason to buy any other domain address, like .org or .me, but I could be mistaken about that. *As with almost every bit of advice I offer in this book, if your instinct tells you there's a better way to do things, by all means go with your gut. Prove me wrong! And if you do, I'd love to hear how you did it.*

---

2. Next, start a Wordpress or Tumblr account. This is the blog site that is going to host the domain you just bought.

3. Next, hire a web designer. I know, I know, I've said that production values don't matter. This is the exception. Having navigated a million badly designed websites, I've come to the conclusion that hiring a designer to make sure that you've got excellent user interface in the form of properly placed links and buttons is a worthwhile investment. This is the one place where I'm telling you to spend money. You want to create content from a home base, and all this networking is to get new "customers" into the "store." If it doesn't look like a nice store or the products aren't on the proper shelves, you won't convert, no matter how much hustle and sweat you put in. Imagine spending nine hundred hours promoting the new store opening and then thousands of people showing up but sales were lackluster. It's because your design was not on point.

A service like this will cost you some cash (1–5k), but if you're on a budget, don't sweat it. Don't put off launching your site just because you can't afford a designer. Start for free and customize later once you can afford it.

If you use Wordpress, there are tons of free Wordpress "themes," or site designs to choose from. I still think a professional designer will give you a better look and feel, but the Wordpress themes are very good.

4. If you're filming a video blog, buy the $150 Flip Cam—something small and light, preferably high definition (HD), that you can use anytime, anywhere you're inspired.

5. Create a Facebook fan page.

6. Open a Twitter account with your domain name.

7. If you're doing video, open a TubeMogul account. If you're doing a written blog, sign up for Ping.fm.

8. Start pumping out content. Let's say you're charismatic and have good screen presence and decide to do a series of videos called Fun Facts from the CPA. Every night you post a video of yourself explaining tax rules in your unique, informative, entertaining way, educating your audience yet also revealing why you are passionate about what some might think a dry, esoteric subject. Talk about whatever you like, as long as it doesn't get you in trouble with your parent company. For example, explain how the recent change in the presidential administration might affect

the ordinary taxpayer. What really happens if a person misses the April 15 deadline? What strategic fiscal issues should a small company consider before deciding to grow? Put as much content out there as you can. There are people in your field who will hate you because you'll be offering up information for free for which they often charge. That's okay. When viewers need accounting help, whom are they going to want to do business with, the guys who hoarded information or the person who proved himself to be open and honest and generous?

Find a way to incorporate some personal stories and details into your posts. Use anecdotes from your own life to illustrate concepts. Let your personality shine so that eventually people who have no need for accounting information are coming to hear you just because it's you.

9. Tweet or post your content via Ping.fm or TubeMogul to distribute it to all of your chosen platforms.

10. Go to Search.Twitter and start searching accounting terms, like "taxes," "401(k)," "accounts payable," and anything else that might be relevant to your blog topic. Start following many of these, keeping in mind that Twitter does not allow you to follow more than 10 percent of the people who are following you, or better yet, @reply them publicly.

11. Next, go to Blogsearch.Google.com (or go to Google, click on "More," and choose "Blogs" from the pull-down menu). Start typing in general terms, like "taxes" and "filing," and search all the obvious keywords. For every blog where you find a mention of these terms, you're going to leave a comment and your name, which should be linked to your homepage.

12. Search the term "accountant" on Facebook. Click on the

tab for "All Results," then click on "Pages." There are hundreds of fan pages, some with nine members, some with thousands. Join as many active ones as possible, but make sure to keep track of them all. When you're done, hit the tab for "Groups" and do the same thing. Although I don't recommend creating your own group, there's no reason you shouldn't get your name on any pre-existing ones that are relevant to your passion.

13. Rinse and repeat.

You will do steps 5 and 8 through 12 over and over and over again for as long as your brand exists. If that sounds tedious or repetitive, just close this book and go do your best to enjoy the life you've got because you're not cut out for this. If you're willing to hustle, though, you'll find you don't get tired of the hunt because every conversation you start up is another opportunity to talk about something you love more than anything else. What's boring about that?

a few additional steps

1. Don't forget to include a list of all of your social network links (such as Twitter.com/GaryVee) on your e-mail signature, letterhead, and business cards.

2. Make sure you have a big fat button on your site that says, "Want to Do Business with Me?" or something along those lines.

We're thinking of this brand building as a marathon, not a sprint, right? So right now, that button will just be there as a reminder of where you're ultimately going with your brand. It's unlikely you're going to get biz dev offers right off the bat, but you never know. More likely, as you build your community you will see the following progression:

- Enthusiastic fans
- Free product offers from businesses that notice your growing fan base
- Biz dev deals from individuals smart enough to see they need to do business with you while you're still affordable

One of my favorite mantras is "Anything is better than zero," but true to my contradictory nature, let me just say that the longer you hold out to monetize your blog, the better. Everyone's financial situation is different and you may feel compelled to take some of the first offers you get, from advertisers, for example. Try to wait, not just because the stronger and bigger your audience, the more cash you can demand when the time is right, but because as soon as you start focusing on monetizing, by necessity you will start to pay less attention to your content and your community.

When you're ready, though, the opportunities to monetize your personal brand will blow your mind.

eleven

start monetizing

Up until now you've been focusing on building your brand by creating killer content and getting that content some traction by building your community one e-mail, one comment, one tweet, one status update at a time. Once you feel you've grown to a point where your brand is sticky and your audience has made your content a regular, even necessary, part of their community and their online experience, you can start to actively create revenue streams. Unlike in the beginning, when you threw out a big net into a big pond to capture in as many members of the social media school of fish as possible, you're now going to drop in your line to a variety of smaller ponds. Be patient. In time, if you continue to hustle, you'll grow your presence and improve your skills to the point where the fish—really, really big fish—will be jumping straight into your hands.

Some revenue ponds to consider include the following.

advertising

A lot has been made of the fact that magazines and newspapers are being crippled because companies are pulling their ads to save money during this recession. Well, of course they are; the cost of radio, magazine, and newspaper advertising space is not in line with the returns in today's world. But companies need to sell if they're going to stay alive, which means that even if their budgets are somewhat smaller than they used to be, they have to spend money to remind consumers they exist. If they want to sell a product, they have to advertise. The difference now is that they're not going to waste their money by throwing it against the wall and seeing what sticks. There are hundreds of billions of dollars in ad revenue out there that need a place to go, and they're winding up online because it's the best return on investment advertisers can find. Remember, where people—consumers—go, money follows, and the people are spending more and more time in the blogosphere. If there's an active, energetic, passionate community spending time on your blog, there is no reason on Earth why advertisers wouldn't want to spend a portion of all that ad revenue there, too.

For example, you're Sally Gardener from upstate New York. You've decided to monetize your passion—vegetable gardens. You've left comments and started conversations with thousands of other avid gardeners and gained some traction as the most expert and entertaining vegetable gardener online. You're good. Really good. People who couldn't tell the difference between a sprig of parsley and cilantro have come to your site to watch the episode where you use a water pistol to defend your last tomato from a hungry squirrel, only to lose the tomato to his partner in crime lurking behind you in the shadows.

Your first instinct when thinking of ways to bring dollars to your site might be to sign up for something like Google AdSense, which allows you to post Google advertisements related to your topic. I'm not a big fan of these because it distracts from your content and makes your page look cheap and cluttered. It also doesn't pay that well. I'm disappointed that so many good bloggers have become dependent on it—there are far more creative avenues to pursue.

Here's a better idea: #1—classy banner ads (à la decknet-work.net), which appear at the top or bottom of your site (don't overdo it!). #2—Go to Google.com, search your subject matter, and check every blog and website to see which companies pay for Google AdSense ads to be posted. Cold-call every relevant company that is buying space on Google AdSense—they're already spending the ad money on the Web, why not spend it on you? You can find a video on this topic on GaryVaynerchuk.com: http://garyvaynerchuk.com/search/cold+call.

speaking engagements

Next, start taking steps to get on the lecture circuit. Have you any idea how many gardening conferences and flower shows go on every week in this country? Come up with an original theme or topic, call the show's coordinators, and offer to give a talk for free. What does that get you? The same social equity as you get with your fantastic online content. It gives you a chance to (a) talk about what you love, (b) build cred, and (c) do it in front of an interested audience, one of whom might be the coordinator for another conference or garden show and who, after seeing you talk, might be compelled to pay you to speak at their venue. As for the conference where you just offered up your services for free, it may take five or six times, but if you're any good at what you do, your audience will start expecting you to appear at these events, and the conference will eventually be willing, even happy, to pay you. It might take a while to get to that point, but you're patient. Right?

affiliate programs

You could also consider doing an affiliate program. This is where you put a link on your site to another site that sells garden products, for example, and if someone clicks through and buys, you get a commission. This can make you some sweet cash. Think about it—a 20 percent commission of a $3,000 prefab greenhouse is $600. And what did you have to do to earn it? Not a whole lot. A good resource for affiliate marketing programs is Commission Junction. Amazon, too, has an extremely popular affiliate program, and there are many others. Just do a Google search for "affiliate programs" to find them.

One of my favorite websites is loaded with affiliates but manages to do it in a truly classy way. Check out www.uncrate.com.

One way I'd love to see more people create revenue is to create their own affiliate deal with another local business. Sally Gardener could call a local nursery and hook up a deal where she gets 10 percent of every click-through and sale to their website from her blog. For those of you who worry that this seems like selling out or mercenary, you shouldn't put anything on your blog that you don't believe in. Therefore, you're not going to do an affiliate with a company whose product you wouldn't buy yourself. In fact, one way to defuse any criticism for allowing ads or affiliate links onto your blog is to include an explanation on your site as to why you're willing to support these particular companies. If you're honest about why you believe in the product and why you've decided to allow selling opportunities on your blog, most people won't be put off. Besides, society is getting used to product placement in movies and television; I expect we'll be seeing more of it in all forms of media.

retail

Develop a product to sell, such as great gardening gloves, decorative objects, soaps, mosquito repellant, whatever you love and think you can do better than anyone else. Even more fun, sell schwag. Create a T-shirt for five bucks and sell it for ten. If you've got ten thousand readers or viewers, and maybe a thousand buy it, that's five grand, and it cost you almost nothing to produce. Plus, now you've got people wearing or using or displaying something with your blog name and address, giving you free marketing and word of mouth.

articles

Hit up online and print magazines and other blogs about contributing articles. If they aren't interested in paying you, offer to reciprocate by mentioning them on your blog. Approach food-and-nutrition nonprofits about writing for their newsletters. Talk to your local farmer's market about contributing to their publication or blog if they don't already have one.

seminars

Invite people to come out and garden with you and give them a chance to ask questions. Your first lessons will go for a relatively low rate, but as word gets around that you're good and that people are seeing results in their gardens after working with you, your rates can go up. Make it an event to broaden your appeal—team up with a local chef who is also building a personal brand. Once the gardening portion of the day is done, everyone joins together to cook a terrific vegetarian lunch. Invite someone from the local food bank to give a talk about how and where people can donate food they grow in their gardens. Coordinate field trips for local schools to come spend their morning with you.

books and tv

It's almost a cliché to remind you that good blogging can lead to book deals. From tackling every recipe in the first volume of

Julia Child's *Mastering the Art of French Cooking* to a satirical list of Stuff White People Like or a collection of photographs of crazy, gross food (This Is Why You're Fat), blogs have long been a hot commodity in the publishing world and have proven their potential as bestsellers. Video blogs, too, have led to TV opportunities. Amanda Congdon, who got her start video blogging and hosting Rocketboom, has appeared on many TV shows (for a while she had a deal with ABC and HBO though it looks like that didn't work out); Perez Hilton, celebrity blogger, had his own reality show and continues to appear on TV. Andy Samberg was a cult Internet hit with his comedy troupe Lonely Island before becoming a star of *Saturday Night Live*.

consulting

As your audience grows and your blog starts to get real attention in the form of media coverage, ad revenue, and requests for speaking at functions, expect to start getting requests for tips and advice from many other gardening bloggers. At first you'll want to offer your time for free, but if you're sitting on a heavy knowledge base, you should eventually start to charge for your time. If you come across as legit and honest, people will respond favorably, especially since you have now "lived it."

How would this process look if your passion were board games?

Pretty cool, actually.

1. Start a video blog called Board Game TV.

2. Send out an e-mail to everyone in your address book asking if you can borrow every game they have in their attic.

3. Review every game. Examine the packaging, the origins of the game, things you like about it, things you don't like, the history of the game.

4. Post it with an eBay affiliate link for the game. You'll get a commission every time someone buys from the link.

5. Do that for several months, making a little money.

6. Launch Collector Friday where you talk about a valuable or rare game you don't even own, maybe one that's up for sale. Interview the person selling it.

7. Knock the hell out of your content for a few months and it's entirely possible that someone from *The Today Show* is going to ask you to talk about board games or your blog on their program.

8. Suddenly, you get a call from Parker Brothers asking if you'll talk at their convention or be their spokesperson.

It could happen. Heck, it will happen.

advertising redux

Anyone who is able to build a gardening show with ten thousand viewers is perfectly justified in reaching out to the big boys. All you have to do is buy a stack of gardening magazines, flip through the pages to see who advertises, and then Twitter or Facebook status out, "Hey, BMW, why are you spending fifty grand on a full-page ad in *Home and Garden* and getting little return on your investment when you could place something with me for just a couple of g's and get crazy ROI?"

create some hoopla

There's one more thing you can do, but it takes a very particular kind of DNA to pull it off. Launch your site. Put out a few days' worth of killer content. Pick up the phone and call big corporate advertising agencies and tell them what you've just done. Explain to them how your expertise and your passion are going to make this thing huge. Tell them you're giving them an incredible chance to buy out the show for the next year while you're still unknown. In a year you'll be able to sell space for three grand an episode, but since you need the money now you're looking for someone to invest and grow with you. Show support today, and you'll repay them with undying loyalty through the course of your career.

Sounds outrageous? I'm telling you, that play is in play somewhere. Ten people reading this book will be able to pull it off. When you do, let me know at gary@vaynermedia.com.

As you can see, there is lots of money to be made, albeit in dribs and drabs to begin, by siphoning off money from already-existing sources.

Some ponds I've mentioned are shallower than others and might not give you the kind of return you dream about right away—fifty bucks here, three hundred there. But how much is your blog earning you now? Nothing? And you're going to turn away fifty bucks?

Say it with me: Anything is better than zero.

That doesn't mean you should do anything to earn a buck, but neither should you walk away from dollars if you don't have any. Too many people think they're big shots when they're nothing in the grand scheme of things. Don't drink your own Kool-Aid, it will negatively impact your business decisions. Even if your ambitions are huge, start slow, start small, build gradually, build smart. The money will be there, and more important, so will the opportunities.

twelve

---

roll with it

You know I like contradiction, so it shouldn't surprise you that one of the most important concepts I want you to keep in mind is diametrically opposed to some of the ideas I've shared with you until now.

I've repeated over and over that in order to build a winning business you have to go whole hog with your passion. True. I've said that if you don't plan ahead and decide exactly what you want and where you want to see your business end up, you're broken. Still true. But what is also true is that as committed and obsessed and goal oriented as entrepreneurs need to be, they also have to be willing to practice what I call "reactionary business," which at heart is about being willing and able to adapt and change. This is where most companies and businesspeople lose the game, by refusing to admit their mistakes or neglecting to look ahead to see what could negatively impact their business. Nothing in life ever goes exactly the way you think it will, and that goes for all of your carefully planned entrepreneurial dreams and goals. Reactionary business allows you to make a couple of crucial moves when the landscape starts to change.

be ready to adapt

You'd be surprised at how many entrepreneurs aren't good at adjusting to changing environments, and it's a major reason why so many businesses don't achieve their full potential. I see it all the time. Someone with ambition and talent decides she's going to be the Martha Stewart of kid-friendly sandwiches, and then all of a sudden discovers that somewhere along the way she reached a core group of beer-drinking dudes who are religiously watching the show. Instead of embracing that demographic and adapting, she refuses to acknowledge it and keeps making fish-shaped pimento cheese. Maybe she does fine with her blog catering to the kiddie set, but can you imagine how much bigger this ambitious person's business could have been if she had given up a day a week to prepare sandwiches perfect for tailgate parties?

A perfect real-life example of a brand that drew an unnecessary line in the sand regarding its positioning is Cristal. Starting in the late 1990s, the upscale Champagne was enthusiastically adopted by the hip-hop community. But instead of embracing and leveraging the attention, the managing director indicated in an interview with the *Economist* that he'd prefer to distance his brand from rappers and their fans, saying, "We can't forbid people from buying it. I'm sure Dom Perignon or Krug would be delighted to have their business." He had the chance to cultivate a golden opportunity to capture major market share and instead he killed it, because smart and influential entertainers like Jay-Z were rightfully offended by the guy's attitude and organized an effective boycott against the brand.

put out fires

Now, reactionary business has nothing to do with social media—everyone in business should practice it even if they've decided to completely ignore social networks (a stupid idea but one that a lot of established brands are following). On the other hand, all of these social networking platforms turbo-boost your ability to be reactionary, not only by enabling you to guide your brand to where it naturally fits or where you discover pockets of interest, but by giving you a lot of power to put out fires. For example, I was seen all over ESPN after the NFL draft booing the Mark Sanchez pick by the New York Jets. It looked like I was hating on the pick and the player, which wasn't true. I didn't know the details of the trade and when I saw the team go from seventeen to five in the rankings, I assumed that the Jets had given up a whole lot to get Sanchez, and that's what was bothering me. Turns out that wasn't the case. Regardless, I felt bad that everyone, including Mark Sanchez if he happened to be watching, misunderstood my reaction. Five years ago I couldn't have fixed the misperception, but thanks to social media, the Monday after the game I was able to use my biggest platform, Wine Library TV, to clarify what I thought.

A more relevant example can be found in the way Domino's used YouTube to respond to the negative publicity they suffered after two employees shot video of themselves doing

disgusting things with the food before serving it to customers. A lot of people pointed to that story as evidence of the
downside to social media because two idiots were able to blast
a negative image of a company out to thousands of consumers within minutes. But the Domino's brand didn't get hurt.
Anyone with half a brain knows that morons work everywhere and that this could happen in any restaurant, from fast
food to reservations only. No one wants people messing with
their food, and of course the employees responsible should
be punished, but their actions didn't hurt the brand. In fact,
I think Domino's helped their brand by showing great reactionary business instincts. I respect how fast they got into the
trenches and responded via the same medium as the crime
that was committed, with a YouTube video. Good for CEO
Patrick Doyle, who in his address appears to be a pretty traditional corporate guy gamely trying to fight fire with fire
(next time, Mr. Doyle, try to look into the camera and lose
the script; it makes a big difference). CEOs and business managers don't need to have a power meeting with their PR department to discuss how to handle a problem like this one;
they should know what they want to say, and then say it. Suc-
cessfully dealing with a situation like this is all about speed,
honesty, and transparency.

I saw this as a great opportunity for Domino's to flip this situation on its head. They, and every other fast-food restaurant,
should open up their kitchens to a livestream that anyone can
watch from anywhere, including while waiting in line to order
pizza. To me, adapting in this way to the reality that cell phones
and Flip Cams (which are going to merge, wait and see) are

always going to make their way behind the scenes of any restaurant would be an outstanding example of reactionary business.

shape your story

Thanks to social networking platforms, your story is going to get told, unfiltered, whether you like it or not. You can no longer control the message, but that's not a bad thing unless you work for a closed-minded PR company. As far as I'm concerned, the biggest hurdle for most corporate brands today is their dependence on their PR people. They're terrified of the unfiltered message, but what they should do is encourage it. Every employee of every company should have a Facebook account where they can talk about their work and the company (in addition to whatever else they want). Let people gripe, let them air their frustrations. Don't wait for exit interviews to find out what your staff really thinks; tap into the pulse of the company and start making changes right away. Yes, there are websites dedicated to allowing people to air their dirty laundry, but people should be allowed to hang their dirty laundry on their own clothesline. Empowering your employees to communicate is a great thing. If you suppress their urge to talk, you're only weakening your brand from within by limiting your access to information.

When you know what people are saying and thinking about your brand, you can address it. If you see falsehood, you can correct it. If you see praise, you can show appreciation. If you see confusion, you can inform. Your empowerment doesn't stop with your staff or your customers, either. It used to be that you were at the mercy of the media, with no say in how it told your story unless it was willing to pick up on your version. If you didn't like the picture it painted, you were kind of stuck. Now you can fight the media itself with these tools, with your blog and Facebook and Twitter. Now you can do a live press conference on Ustream, whereas ten years ago you could try but it was always a gamble whether someone would show up with a TV camera.

trendspotting

Some entrepreneurs are really into creating the next big thing. Not me. I'm about identifying the next big thing and jumping all over it. To me, honing your ability to act on waxing and waning social and cultural trends is a major reactionary business move.

Some people are born with good trendspotting intuition. My whole life I've been able to see something and just feel that it's going to be big. I felt it for baseball cards, for toy collectibles, for wine, for the Internet and video blogging, and I'm sure I'll see the next trend that comes around. I look everywhere for inspiration. Recently I noticed that certain kids are using markers to draw tattoos on themselves and create body graffiti. Occasionally I've used my forty-five-minute drive to work to wonder, what does it mean that kids are drawing their own tattoos? How do I capitalize on it? Where is the opportunity? Then while on the Thunder Cruise (a cruise for my fans) in April, we docked in the Bahamas and I noticed a huge line at the kids' tattoo station at the Atlantis. If I were in the ink business, I'd want to create an organic, nontoxic, kid-friendly, skin-friendly brand of ink and capture the market of kids who want to design their own tattoos. The tremendous line at the booth told me that parents are clearly ready for this. I'm not the right guy to invent the product to fill that market need, but if you do it, let me know.

Being reactionary means that you're always thinking about the meaning behind cultural change. Let's say you're at a party and a friend tells you she's canceling cable. You hear that and your radar should go off. Canceling cable? No one would have canceled cable two years ago, what's going on? If you haven't figured it out already, I'll tell you why it's important: it means that the day is almost here when there will be no difference between watching TV and watching online video. Cable on Demand and Netflix and TiVo and YouTube and Hulu have each pushed the envelope a little farther by extending the life of movies and shows and by making network programming schedules irrelevant, but the next phase will be even more dramatic. Eventually Comcast or Time Warner is going to announce a new channel that airs online videos. You'll be able to use your remote to search by subject. Now the kid who draws tattoos on his arm will be able to type in "body graffiti" and find forty-five different shows about body art on the Internet. He's going to create his own TV watching experience, not just swallow what the TV stations have decided to feed him. If you happen to host a graffiti video blog that at first was reaching five thousand people, you're suddenly going to have the potential to reach hundreds of thousands. For someone practicing reactionary business—someone who is looking ahead and adapting to markets and taking advantage of new opportunities to communicate—that puts a lot of media dollars into play.

Thanks to social networking we now have access to powerful, real-time, streamlined data that can allow us to steer our ships very accurately in response to trends and to turn challenges into huge opportunities. But reactionary business isn't limited to businesses developed through social media platforms. Whatever the next business phenomenon turns out to be, your reactionary business skills will be critical to capitalizing on it.

thirteen

---

legacy is greater than currency

I t used to be that only people in the public eye had to worry about controlling their message. They used teams of stylists and publicists to shape their image, and even the media acted more as a guardian than a snitch—no one knew about our presidents' affairs or an actor's drug habit or a tycoon's back-room deals. Those days are long gone, not just for celebrities but for all of us. We're all in the public eye now, swimming around in a clear glass fish bowl of our own making. With every e-mail and video and blog post and tweet and status update, we add to the real-time documentary of our lives. For the person who thinks of himself or herself as a brand—and remember, everyone needs to start thinking of themselves as a brand—the ability to spread your great ideas and share your triumphs is a golden opportunity. The downside to this, of course, is that when you mess up or things go wrong, there's no longer anywhere to hide. The public can be forgiving when it wants to be, but rather than test its generosity, I urge you to start training yourself to think through the consequences of every business decision you make before you actually make it.

Perhaps that sounds like obvious advice, but I know for a fact that many people have a hard time thinking long term. Successful entrepreneurs are like good chess players; they can imagine the various possibilities ahead and how each one will trigger their next move. Too many people, however, can't think past their first move (worse, some don't care to, like a small number of CEOs who know they'll be gone in three years and just want the stock price to go up no matter the long-term impact on the company). They're all about what's good for their business today. That kind of thinking is at the root of a lot of really crap judgment calls, the kind that will sink a personal brand. Achieving 100 percent happiness is the whole point of living your passion, of course, but to my mind that happiness is unachievable if you don't recognize that with every decision you make, you're building more than just a business, you're building a legacy.

For all of us made of ambitious, competitive, hungry DNA, the urge to take our personal brands as far as they will go is second nature. But let me assure you that if you're coming exclusively from the monetizing angle, you're going to lose. How you build your business is so much more important than how much you make while doing it. Yes, I want to buy the Jets. Yes, I intend to crush it. But as I build my brand and make money and work to achieve my goals, I am always hyperaware that everything I'm doing is being recorded for eternity. It does bother me a little that all the cursing I sometimes do in my keynotes is going to become part of my story, yet I have to embrace it because that's just how my DNA expresses itself when I'm onstage. I want to be proud of what I do. I want my kids and my grandkids and great-grandkids to be proud of me. This is why every decision I make is weighed in terms of currency and legacy. Will this business deal make me money? Yes? Good. Will I be proud of how I made that money? Yes? Okay, then, let's do this. If the answer is no, I don't go there, ever. Legacy always wins.

My obsession with legacy should explain to you why I insist on trying to answer every e-mail, tweet, ping, or comment. Back in the early days I used to reply within a couple of hours. Now the volume of my correspondence has gotten so overwhelming that it takes me a few months to get back to people, but I guarantee you, I always try to. If I realize I'm falling behind because I'm busy or I have a brutal travel schedule, I'll shoot off a short video explaining what's going on and promise to reply to everyone as soon as possible.

Now, a lot of people think I'm out of my mind for keeping this up. In the beginning they thought it was kind of cute, but now they think I'm insane. After all, I'm on the social network radar. I may be only a triple-Z list celebrity, but it would be fair to say that I've done all right for myself and that I've secured an interested, loyal audience through my particular brand of perseverance and hard work. Surely, some well-meaning friends have suggested, people would understand if I had to delegate my correspondence or even start picking and choosing who gets a personal reply.

That's not how it works. Not in my world, anyway. No matter how big you get, every e-mail, every customer, every friend, every single person with whom you come into contact matters and deserves respect and attention. Not because you never know who's going to be a good contact or resource later on, although that's definitely true, but just because. If someone takes the time to reach out to you, it's your obligation to reciprocate.

That said, the truth is that my e-mail volume is getting to the point where I fear I may have to make some adjustments in how I respond to correspondence, but rest assured that I will find a way to remain accessible to my friends and fans.

Legacy is the mortar of successful, lasting brands. I've known this since my days in retail. There was one year where I found out that a customer in Westchester, New York, hadn't received her case of White Zinfandel. It was December 22 and there was no way FedEx was going to deliver the wine in time for Christmas. My ordering department had received the complaint, but because the customer was neither a regular nor the order particularly large, they hadn't brought it to my attention. By the time I got wind of the problem there was only one thing left to do. I threw a case of White Zinfandel in my car and drove three hours in blinding snow to the woman's house. Did I mention that she lived in another state? That it was our busiest time of the year? That my time was much more valuable in the store during those six round-trip hours? And believe me, there was no angle. The customer was an older woman who lived far away and wasn't about to start hosting a lot of parties and using us as her exclusive wine supplier.

Yet I knew that it was up to me to set the tone at the store, and that this was a perfect way to do it. Our corporate culture was cemented the day I delivered the case of wine to that woman. I follow the same philosophy when I answer every single one of my e-mails. Making connections, creating and continuing meaningful interaction with other people, whether in person or in the digital domain, is the only reason we're here. Remember that, set the tone, and build legacy.

conclusion

the time is now, the message is forever

Today's entrepreneurs are building on top of a foundation that has changed our society forever, something that goes much deeper than Twitter and Tumblr and YouTube. The greatest paradox surrounding the Internet is that as much as it allows us to isolate and limit ourselves only to what we believe is immediately relevant to our specific needs, so does it allow us to connect at unprecedented levels and extend ourselves beyond our farthest horizons. People still underestimate the reach of this thing. The Internet is only fourteen years old or so—it's so young it hasn't even had sex—yet it has already crushed many of the biggest communication platforms known to humankind, and it's not done. The Internet is as powerful as oxygen, but we have not seen its full capabilities. It's got a long way to go, and it's going to morph and change and reveal all kinds of surprises. You've got to be prepared to evolve and adapt along with it.

Whatever you do, don't read this book and take everything I say word for word. I've offered you a blueprint of the step-by-step process of taking advantage of what the Internet has to offer you now, which has worked well for me. But in six months the environment will have changed again. If you see something—a platform, a trend, a social pattern that makes your radar go off, you should absolutely follow it. Don't ever be afraid to put your feet in that water, whether I've said a word about it or not. Listen to your DNA—it will always lead you in the right direction.

If there's any message I want you to take away, it's that true success—financial, personal, and professional—lies above all in loving your family, working hard, and living your passion. In telling your story. In authenticity, hustle, and patience. In caring fiercely about the big and the small stuff. In valuing legacy over currency. Social media is an important part of it for now, but maybe it won't always be. These concepts, however, are forever, no matter what the next business platform or social phenomenon turns out to be.

appendix a:
did you forget anything?

I thought it would be helpful to provide a checklist of all the steps you want to take as you build your personal brand:

1. Identify your passion.
2. Make sure you can think of at least fifty awesome blog topics to ensure stickiness.
3. Answer the following questions:
   - Am I sure my passion is what I think it is?
   - Can I talk about it better than anyone else?
4. Name your personal brand. You don't have to refer to it anywhere in your content, but you should have a clear idea of what it is. For example, "The no-bs real-estate agent," "The connoisseur of cookware," "The cool guide to young-adult books boys will love to read."

5. Buy your user name—.com and .tv, if possible—at GoDaddy.com.

6. Choose your medium: video, audio, written word.

7. Start a Wordpress or Tumblr account.

8. Hire a designer.

9. Include a Facebook Connect link, Call-to-Action buttons, Share Functions, and a button that invites people to do business with you in a prominent place on your blog.

10. Create a Facebook fan page.

11. Sign up for Ping.fm or TubeMogul and select all of the platforms to which you want to distribute your content. Choosing Twitter and Facebook is imperative; the others you can select according to your needs and preference.

12. Post your content.

13. Start creating community by leaving comments on other people's blogs and forums and replying to comments to your own comment.

14. Use Twitter Search (or Search.Twitter) to find as many people as possible talking about your topic, and communicate with them.

15. Use Blogsearch.Google.com to find more blogs that are relevant to your subject.

16. Join as many active Facebook fan pages and groups relating to your blog topic as possible.

17. Repeat steps 12 through 16 over and over and over and over and over.

18. Do it again.

19. And again.

20. When you feel your personal brand has gained sufficient attention and stickiness, start reaching out to advertisers and begin monetizing.
21. Enjoy the ride.

appendix b:
five business ideas i won't get to—
they're yours

I believe that livestreaming is the future, so most of the new businesses I envision build on that platform. Here are a few that I will unfortunately not be able to get around to, even though I think they have tremendous potential. See what you can do with them.

the QVC of the internet

It blows my mind that this hasn't been done on a serious level yet. Ustream.tv and Justin.tv are free platforms that replicate live television—they provide the perfect opportunity for a great salesperson to start an efficient online QVC. Find a terrific host (or host the show yourself), mix things up by inviting guests—

inventors, entrepreneurs, authors—and talk about whatever you find interesting or useful or exciting. You don't even need vendor relationships to start this up—just affiliate link all of the products you think are worth selling. Eventually vendors will be begging to get airtime on your show. In addition, you wouldn't need a call center to handle customers and sales. While you or your host talked about a product, a box would appear at the bottom of the screen with a button allowing people to start clicking through to make their purchase. Needless to say you'd have an archive and break products into categories so that shoppers could easily find past episodes and shop to their hearts' content.

a tea blog

I think the tea market in the United States is about to blow up, and for the person who wants to educate and entertain the masses there will be enormous opportunity to build a site much like Wine Library TV. Offer a tea-of-the-month club and you'll be in serious business.

the sports center of the web

Where is the twenty-four-hour online sports-talk show? I totally see this as a college play—five to ten college seniors debating sports while livestreaming on Ustream.tv from a dorm room. Obviously you couldn't compete with the likes of ESPN, who can purchase the right to use sports highlight reels, but you could certainly give radio stations a major run for their money. Build up a few major personalities to draw regular viewers. I would love to see two brothers (I wish AJ and I could find the time to do this!) do an online call-in twenty-four-hour sports-talk show, much like ESPN's Mike and Mike, or even the longtime hit in New York, Mike and the Mad Dog. Or become the online world's Don Imus. Advertisers would eat up the chance to get their name mentioned on a show with a hundred thousand listeners and viewers. Imagine: "This hour brought to you by Sports Authority." Has a nice ring to it, right?

online book reviews

This one has my panties in a bunch big-time. All you independent bookstores screaming that book lovers should bring you their business because you can offer more personal attention and knowledge, even if you can't compete on price? Here's your chance to swat the big boys down: a daily book review video blog. Get two or three of your most entertaining, most passionate associates to talk about the books they love, what's coming up, what's hot, what's not. At the same time, lower the price on your one hundred top-selling books. Spread your neighborhood charm to the world. By using your blog to expand your reach beyond your local market, you will explode your brand and your business.

pepsilandhousplace.com

What the heck is this? Just an example of the kind of destination url a big corporation might launch to get a fire under their brand. If I were a brand manager (I'd love to say a CEO would get on this, but brand managers are usually the ones in the trenches), I'd create a one-off website to leverage interest in my brand, where consumers can go for information and even samples. It is completely separate from the homepage and allows you to track your campaign and how much effect it's having. You're thinking you've seen special sites for brands before. Not like this you haven't, because this one would bring the power of Facebook into play, too. Build a fan page for your brand announcing a game or contest that gets people to start interacting with your brand. By participating, they get free samples and other perks. Combing the reach of Facebook with product sampling is something that very few, if any, companies are doing, and it's about time they start.